The Wounded Leader

Richard H. Ackerman
Pat Maslin-Ostrowski

The Wounded Leader

How Real Leadership Emerges
in Times of Crisis

JOSSEY-BASS
A Wiley Company
San Francisco

Published by Jossey-Bass
A Wiley Imprint
989 Market Street, San Francisco, CA 94103-1741   www.josseybass.com

Jossey-Bass books and products are available through most bookstores. To contact Jossey-Bass directly call our Customer Care Department within the U.S. at 800-956-7739, outside the U.S. at 317-572-3986, or fax 317-572-4002.

Jossey-Bass also publishes its books in a variety of electronic formats. Some content that appears in print may not be available in electronic books.

Library of Congress Cataloging-in-Publication Data

Ackerman, Richard H., date–
    The wounded leader : how real leadership emerges in times of
crisis / Richard H. Ackerman, Pat Maslin-Ostrowski.—1st ed.
        p. cm.—(The Jossey-Bass education series)
Includes bibliographical references and index.
    ISBN 0-7879-6110-8 (hard : alk. paper)
    1. School administrators—United States—Case studies.
2. Educational leadership—United States—Case studies.
I. Maslin-Ostrowski, Pat, date– II. Title. III. Series.
    LB2831.82.A34 2002
    371.2'011—dc21   2002001388

Printed in the United States of America
FIRST EDITION
HB Printing   10 9 8 7 6

The Jossey-Bass Education Series

For the wounded leader

Contents

Preface

No man hath affliction enough that is not matured,
and ripened by it.

John Donne

The Wounded Leader is the result of many courageous conversations. It is a work in progress, looking outward at the inevitable crises faced by school leaders and inward at their very personal responses. It seeks to understand how school leaders cope with and respond to significant dilemmas in their practice and what the experience means to them. For several years, we have been listening to the stories of school leaders who have experienced a critical event in their leadership practice. By their accounts, these are experiences of the kind that wounds to the core—what some leaders call their integrity or identity, the soul of a person's way of being. Indeed, these are the most integral aspects of a leadership life.

The book is driven by two interrelated questions. First, how does a reasonable, well-intentioned person, who happens to be a school leader, preserve a healthy and real sense of self in the face of a host of factors challenging that self in the best scenario, and leading to a wounding crisis in the worst? Second, what perspective toward the work of leadership might fortify the impact of these challenges, and produce a mind-set that leaves the person open to learn and grow from such experience? In many respects, *The Wounded Leader* is a way of saying thank you to the school leaders whom we have been fortunate to know and who have lived out these questions through their leadership.

The leadership life, we recognize, is a complex balance of conflicting forces and tension that manages to function most of the time; however, school leadership can take a person from an inspired moment to a crisis in an instant. School is essentially a human event. Things happen unrelentingly, and a leader is expected to know or do something. Yet the nature of events that give rise to wounding is difficult to categorize and predict. The shape of things on the outside does not necessarily correspond to, or even reveal, how the wound looks and feels on the inside. It is, after all and ultimately, a personal matter.

Our conversations with school leaders about dilemma and crisis have ranged over wide territory. Wounding finds its most distinct expression in familiar questions asked at some time or another by beginning and veteran principals alike: How can I be all these things to all these people? How can I know and do all I should? Such questions reflect an endemic state of leadership life in which constant embroilment in the needs of other people and continual decision making in close quarters with people whose hopes ride on the outcome make the work not only draining to one's energy but intellectually, emotionally, and psychically exhausting (Ackerman, Donaldson, and van der Bogert, 1996).

Beneath the surface tension, wounding is often felt at a deeper and more personal level, where a leader's decision, motives, and integrity are impugned by others. Such a response may be signaled by a critical event or a series of events in leadership practice; it need not have anything to do with the leader's genuine competence. In this sense, we have come to understand that wounding feels like an attack on the heart, perhaps like a heart attack, that reflects some of the same characteristics: loss of control, powerlessness, fear, and vulnerability.

Leadership has been described as the capacity to be totally and utterly oneself, to be able to show up fully, to express oneself, and to share this self with an organization that one cares about and wants to influence (Bennis, 1989; Whyte, 2001). If this is the case, then wounding at its worst means leaving the self outside the school, becoming a hollow stranger to oneself and one's leadership altogether. We are concerned that the leaders we describe as wounded are primarily at risk of not feeling that they can be themselves in their leadership, that their ability to see leadership as a personal expression engaging their deepest desire and energy is jeopardized. In essence, leaders should not be mere technicians who leave their individuality at the schoolhouse door. These conditions are not often the subject of books on leadership. Yet they are a significant part of the inner emotional landscape of the leaders and, for better or worse, describe the state of the wounded leader.

The book is ultimately optimistic. It carries an age-old and hopeful premise: that crisis is an emergent occasion for transformation. What is involved in this potential change is the possibility of breaking free of the image of a leader that has been assumed. To really feel that moment is to have a vision of a change to come, usually experienced with intensity and great distress. Sustained and repeated wounding can disrupt lives and schools in seemingly endless ways. Yet most of the leaders we have been privileged to meet were not incapacitated; indeed, many demonstrated the courage to realize where they were, how they got there, and where they were going.

The material of the book is straightforward. It is based on story, and the stories are the result of our conversation with self-described wounded leaders. Although our work is inspired by a medical metaphor, and we borrow liberally from it to make the point, the book is not about illness per se. It is about how school leaders respond to and make sense of their wounds. Arthur Frank (1995), who has written eloquently and sensitively on the subject of illness and narrative, said of wounded people that "their injuries become the source of the potency of their stories" (p. xii). Like the ill person, the wounded leader has an important story to tell. Just as illness is part of life, wounding is an important aspect and source of leadership—any kind of leadership.

The book is informed by a number of works, in several genres, on illness experience (Kleinman, 1988; Frank, 1991) and further relies on the metaphor of the ill person as a "wounded storyteller" (Frank, 1995). Thus the stories, as well as our interpretation, are situated in a generative understanding of narrative. Story and narrative are central to the kind of work leaders do—leadership that takes seriously the quest for meaning of one's own leadership.

We have listened not only for the explicit content—that is, the actions, events, and responses—but for the story the person is telling herself as well. We listen for how the tale finds a way back to the emotional moment of engagement, which requires the risk of letting all of oneself really show in leadership. In doing so, we listen again for who the person becomes in her story; how she manages to become that person; and whether, if at all, her wound helps in understanding herself and her leadership any better.

An important related theme lies in the larger implications of stories of this kind for leadership itself, and for the place called school where leadership is practiced. Can there be something in the nature of leadership that prevents knowledgeable, skilled, decisive, and well-intentioned people from successfully leading the work of school improvement? Simply put, what is it about leadership that gets in the way of leadership? Although there has been a virtual revolution in medicine concerning how we think about the diseases that now afflict us, this has not been the case in educational leadership. There needs to be better recognition, understanding, and honoring of the myriad ways in which emotion, mind, and personality have an impact on the necessary aspects of leadership, guiding the quality of educational experiences students receive. With commensurate emotional intelligence and reflection in what is often a state of dissonance, a leader can find the opening to grow personally and professionally, adding a critical dimension to leadership capacity. Against a background of leadership theory and practice, which we have been studying and teaching for years, we realize that the voices of these wounded leaders are often left out of the professional dialogue, yet they are an essential part of the leadership landscape.

We bring to the book a strong friendship as students of leadership who have spent professional lives in the field of leadership education, including former lives as a school head, counselor, and most recently professor of educational leadership. Our work takes us into countless schools where we often witness conditions that nullify the chance of real leadership emerging, and we see how achingly fragile and vulnerable leaders can be. Whether in a school, a university classroom, at a professional development workshop, or attending a conference, we are invariably reminded that the personal side of leadership is commonly diminished, stripped of meaning, or forgotten altogether. Listening to our graduate students as well as beginning and veteran leaders talk about a crisis experience, it is easy to feel their frustration in not being able to lead in a way that fulfills them while simultaneously achieving school goals.

The research for this book represents a line of inquiry into leaders and crisis that has taken place over a period of seven years. (See Appendix A for a discussion of research methodology.) Earlier studies that we conducted about how leaders use story to make sense of their practice brought us to the idea of the wounded leader, and we have been preoccupied with this work ever since. The broad objective of our research and this resulting book is to listen our way into the world of school leaders who have experienced a crisis in practice, so that we may understand the meaning of their wounding experience.

Our stance with respect to the conversations that have informed this book, however, is more like the hospice worker who is enjoined to "stay close and do nothing" (Collett, 1997). The challenge for us as researchers has been, at first hand, to understand our own in-volvement with this material and then humbly come to see our-selves primarily as witnesses. As we note in Appendix A, what distinguishes the conversation is the participatory nature of the rela-tionship we established with the sixty-five school leaders. Our real work has been to learn how to give up our own agenda and just lis-ten (Remen, 2000).

This, then, is a book that draws on the work and lives of many in an effort to bring school leaders to greater self-awareness and to further a conversation that must transpire if healing is to occur. We cannot *not* think about the wounds of school leaders. While the reader may find a sometimes subjective and idiosyncratic quality to what we say here, we hope it is a good starting place for further con-versation, speculation, and inquiry. We invite the reader to find him-self in the stories that follow. An eminent Quaker woman, when asked about her relationship to her faith, replied, "It's not often the subject of my conversations, but it tends to guide my steps" (Brin-ton, 1940). So, too, for wounded leaders and their wounds. We believe there is much to be learned following in their footsteps.

The book is divided into three parts. The first sets the stage for leadership wounding. In Chapter One, we describe some of the chronic tensions that characterize life in schools and create a host for wounding. We present three core understandings that form the foundation for the book. Chapter Two describes the meanings of wounding as imbedded in the realms of mythology, medicine, and the person.

Part Two relates the stories of self-described wounded educa-tional leaders. The stories are simple and perhaps profound; they show how, through everyday crises of leadership, there is possibility of life-changing insights that can bring unexpected blessings. With-in these stories, readers may find their own story.

Part Three explores questions raised in the stories and the par-ticular lessons revealed to us. In Chapter Ten, we discuss the place of story in leadership and focus on the wounded leader as wounded storyteller. Chapter Eleven addresses the implications of wounding for leadership preparation and professional development. Chapter Twelve closes the book by offering modest hope for finding a "cure" for leadership wounding in our lifetime.

February 2002   Richard H. Ackerman
                                                   Pat Maslin-Ostrowski

Acknowledgments

As we remember it, the idea of the wounded leader came to us in a conversation several years ago in Edinburgh, Scotland. We had just presented a conference paper on case method teaching and retired to the warm hospitality of a friendly pub, set at the foot of a magnificent craggy mountain with Edinburgh Castle looming above, overlooking the entire city. It is possible that the single malt whiskey and haggis added inspiration to the conversation, but more likely it was simply something we've come to depend upon between us—deep and abiding listening—that led to the intersection of an idea at the right moment when we were ready for a greater perspective. Little did we know then of the territory ahead, that the notion of leadership wounding would dominate our research agenda for the next seven years and take us into countless conversations with family, friends, colleagues, students, leaders, and of course each other. For the two of us, this book is yet another chapter in a friendship that began in graduate school and reflects a deep respect for the differing gifts we each have.

There are many people to thank.

A number of good friends and colleagues happily agreed to review early drafts of this book. They each gave us good honest feedback as well as a vision of possibility in the manuscript. If we were smart enough to take advantage of all their suggestions, they deserve all the credit. In places where we didn't, we accept full responsibility for the omission. Thank you, Gordon A. Donaldson, Jr.; Roland S. Barth; David Hagstrom; Becky van der Bogert; Phil Hunsberger; Joe Richardson; Kathleen Huie; Jennifer Freeland; Jeanethe Thompson; and Robert Magrisso, M.D., whose own wounding experience and wisdom continues to inspire us. We are indebted to Leslie Iura, our editor at Jossey-Bass, who saw the promise of our ideas and stayed the course with us. We are grateful to Tom Finnegan for his elegant and painstaking pruning of our manuscript. We would like to give special thanks to a legion of unnamed school leaders, including principals, heads of schools, and superintendents, who were generous with their stories.

There have been many individuals from our own personal circles who have made contributions to the book, of which they themselves may be unaware. Richard would like to thank University of Massachusetts Lowell colleagues Judy Davidson, Joyce Gibson, Chuck Christensen, Robert Gower, Judith Boccia, and Don Pierson. Richard also thanks members of the Lowell Leadership Academy; Milli Pierce, director of the Principals' Center at the Harvard Graduate School of Education, for letting him test these ideas way back; Jeffrey Hanna, Anthony Amodeo, and the Mid-Hudson Leadership Academy HELP center, for making these ideas a practical reality; John Braman, for his sailing wisdom and more; Bob Wimpelberg, for his intelligent understanding and humor; Brian and Carmen Riedlinger, Debbie Randolph, Scott Bauer, and the fellows and folks at the School Leadership Center of Greater New Orleans, for the music and friendship; Richard Safier, for writing the next book; David Mallery, for spirited listening; Jan Arend Brands, for the constant long-distance conversation; and our good friend Ron Gallo, president and CEO of The Rhode Island Foundation, for being the most wonderful outlier! Richard thanks good old friends Peter Cohen; Robert Perry; Polly Chandler and Greg Chanis; Sarah Smith and Joe Newman; Lola and Mia Bogyo, for not asking if it's done yet too often; and of course, his loyal and extended family, Ellie and Merritt Wilson, Rich and Pamela Cantor, and Mom.

Pat is grateful to Florida Atlantic University students and colleagues John Pisapia, Michele Acker-Hocevar, Ira Bogotch, and David Kumar, for support and encouragement; Raejean Kaplan, for offering a business perspective on wounding; Caryl Frankenberger, for morning inspiration; the memory of Carter Cooper, friend and past president of Web Whispers Nu-Voice Club; Arlene Stathis, for being a lifeline on the home front; Linda Harris-Sicular, for meaningful conversation; Shelagh Ryan Masline, for counsel, along with helpful and incisive comments on various versions of the manuscript; and Eileen Masline, for wisdom, wit, and love.

Finally from Pat: eternal thanks to my daughter, Bridget Maslin Ostrowski, who reminds me why children deserve only the best schools; and to my husband, Bill Ostrowski, with whom one lifetime together is not long enough.

From Richard: to my wife, Bobbi, the true love of my life, whose smile and angelic patience allowed us to survive writing this book, and to our beloved dog Zelda, whose insistence on nature walks created difficult moments of interruption in the writing as well as tremendous reflective breakthroughs and inspiration.

R.H.A.
P.M.O.

The Authors

Richard H. Ackerman, a former school teacher and school head, is currently associate professor of education at the University of Massachusetts Lowell Graduate School of Education and associate in education at the Harvard Graduate School of Education. He is coauthor of *Making Sense as a School Leader: Persisting Questions, Creative Opportunities*, with Gordon Donaldson and Rebecca van der Bogert. He is also coeditor-in-chief of New Directions for School Leadership, a monograph series published by Jossey-Bass and designed to help school leaders sort through ideas and practices. He serves as codirector of the International Network of Principals' Centers, a fifteen-year-old collaboration of professional associations, universities, and education agencies working actively to strengthen leadership at the school level through professional development for leaders. Ackerman is currently involved in exploring psychological and spiritual aspects of leadership. He lives on the north shore of Massachusetts in the town of Magnolia, where he and his wife, Bobbi, and their dog, Zelda, enjoy peaceful ocean living.

Pat Maslin-Ostrowski is associate professor of educational leadership at Florida Atlantic University, where she has been principal investigator for the South Florida Consortium of Schools and director of research. Currently she serves on the Broward Middle School Council and School Facilities Task Force. She has worked in a variety of

educational settings, including a New York middle school, the
Rhode Island Department of Education, the University of Rhode
Island, and Rhode Island College. She holds a B.A. from Syracuse
University, an M.A. and M.Ed. from Columbia University, and
M.Ed. and Ed.D. degrees from the Harvard Graduate School of Edu-
cation. She lives in Parkland, Florida, with her husband, thirteen-
year-old daughter, and four cats.

The Wounded Leader

Part I

Ironic Blessings

1

To the Stars Through Adversity (Ad Astra per Aspera)

Consider Bruce. He had enjoyed nine years of a fulfilling, productive high school principalship, replete with accolades for leading a successful, high-performing school. He was known in the community as a tough but fair and honest principal. People appreciated his constant visibility at school events and his taking the time to know the students. Yet one morning he woke up to find in the local newspaper a scathing letter to the editor, condemning him as a corrupt principal. His whole life suddenly screeched to a halt. An angry parent, who also happened to be a prominent member of the community, was accusing Bruce of manipulating grades so that certain favored athletes could compete in the upcoming semifinals of the football season. Bruce knew he had done no such thing and was deeply disturbed that his ethics were being challenged, especially in this public forum.

He thought the school could move on after he told everyone the truth—that, in fact, the charge was an outrageous lie. The truth apparently was not sufficient. The situation got progressively worse. The letter had unmasked certain questionable practices in the athletic department, and Bruce found himself embroiled in a major controversy. The crisis escalated, with the school board using the incident, in his mind, as a political football. The next thing he knew, agitated parents were storming his office, the superintendent was breathing down his neck, and the story became headline news.

Gone was the interest in exploring the merit of block scheduling; gone was the focus on school improvement; gone was the peaceful, compatible relationship he had established with his faculty and community.

These events consumed Bruce, leaving him with mixed emotions. He feared he was being misunderstood by a number of his constituents. It hurt to have his honesty and integrity wrongly questioned, particularly in a public arena.

As we listened carefully to Bruce's story, it became evident that he was emotionally disconnecting from the people he served and was starting to doubt his own leadership. The defensive, angry person he was becoming did not seem to fit him. Disconnection is, unfortunately, an all-too-common form of wounding that we have witnessed over and over again as we talk to school leaders across the country. Like Bruce, leaders may—or may not—use this crisis as an opening to learn about themselves and their leadership.

Against the backdrop of all the tension and questions surrounding leadership work is a fundamental faith that a leader's influence over a school is healthful for all. In our experience, however, and in the stories of the school leaders such as Bruce whom we have interviewed, most could never anticipate or prepare themselves and others for the events that came their way. Neither could they have a perfect answer, or even a good one, for every problem. Most important, to the extent that they felt out of touch with themselves, people they affected, and people they were affected by, the school leaders felt unable to trust their own leadership. This is the beginning of the wound. It seems to us that the deepest obligation a leader has is to engage continually in a reflective process of making sense of his or her effect on others and on the school, and of understanding personal wounds.

There are inevitable boundaries drawn between professional life and personal life, outer life and inner life, mind and body, illness and health, psyche and spirit, even life and death. Organizations such as schools tend to live with fairly strict boundaries, trying to keep things neat and tidy. But most school leaders recognize that their own lives, and particularly their inner lives, are not like that. This is not to say that boundaries do not serve a useful purpose; they do. If you are a principal, for example, and trying to maintain a reasonable family life, you have to draw boundaries somewhere. Our interest in the wound is not a challenge to all boundaries. But to experience life with a threatening illness, or to experience school life from the perspective of a leadership crisis, is to potentially find oneself crossing boundaries one may have thought impermeable and encountering other boundaries one did not even know were there. For the school leader, the crossing often begins as a significant collision with the organizational environment; it inevitably leads to conflict, anguish, and more. Yet it is precisely in the midst of these environmental and psychic challenges that school leaders may find the meaning of their own wounds.

Chronic Work-Life Tensions

Today, schools and school leaders are caught in a strong riptide. Leadership itself seems increasingly at risk. There is widespread agreement that in the United States schools are facing a dearth of leaders capable of providing good leadership. Constant reports on the shortage of school leaders, as well as concerns regarding the job itself, find more wounded leaders leaving or languishing in the world of schools than ever before. Retirement, the decreasing number of applicants, and inadequate leadership support and development account for some of these conditions (National Association of State Boards of Education, 1999), but not all. School leaders and those aspiring to leadership persistently cite job-related stress and time fragmentation, the growing pressure of high-stakes testing and accountability, and the social problems that schools are assuming in trying to instruct students as major factors influencing their standing (National Association of

Elementary School Principals, 2001). It is not surprising that many school leaders today are increasingly reluctant to assume a job as difficult as leadership has become.

The conditions just described capture some present-day demands and realities affecting the quality of leadership life out there, a life that seems increasingly less sustainable for leaders themselves. Leadership must, among other things, attend well to a school's needs and be healthful and replenishing for those who lead (Ackerman, Donaldson, and van der Bogert, 1996). Nevertheless, there are endemic conditions on the ground floor of most schools that make it challenging for the leader to influence the school positively (as well as maintain it as a healthy place for the leader).

Donaldson (2001) describes some major attributes of schools that contribute to a "leadership-resistant architecture" reflected in what he calls a "conspiracy of busyness" (p. 11). There is, according to Donaldson, little time for the school leader to convene people to plan, organize, and follow through. Contact and the transaction of business often take place catch-as-catch-can. Results from a formal staff meeting may be inadequate, or characterized by competing forces, limited time and energy, and overall lack of quality time. Informal gatherings, Donaldson points out, are the most continual means of communication, but opinion setting and relationship building in schools are mostly inaccessible and even resistant to the principal's formal attempt to guide and structure the direction of the school. Important information is communicated informally and sometimes haphazardly. The larger the school, the more complex and impersonal the environment, and the fewer the opportunities a principal has for individual relationship building or problem solving.

Donaldson concludes that these structural conditions in schools work against the success of classical leadership. Frustrated principals find themselves pressing to get their message across, sometimes making decisions in a way that is counterproductive and fosters resistance. Principals come to be seen for their positional authority, not for their ability to facilitate good practices and policies. These are prime conditions for wounding.

The Story in the Stories

The chronic work-life tension, conditions, and issues facing the school leader today and the resulting personal challenges form the heart of this book. What does it mean to become yourself in your leadership? What are the integral elements school leaders find difficult to face about their relationship to work and their own leadership? How do leaders nurture themselves so they can continue to care for their schools through such demanding work? To what extent does concern with the issues of the wounded leader forecast a new direction for leadership work itself?

A unifying theme of this book, the story within the stories, is this: understanding the meaning of wounding through the prism of the educational leader's experience offers a potentially remarkable path, not only to real leadership but to being a real person in one's leadership. The leadership wound itself represents an extraordinary source of learning and a critical opening to what may be most at stake in the practical exercise of leadership, namely, oneself.

Three core understandings emerge from the stories in this book. The first is that leadership roles often do not support, confirm, or resonate with the psychic needs of the person who becomes a leader. The second is that wounding is an inevitable part of leadership. This leads to the third, that woundedness is a double-edged (at least) sword. A wound has the potential to be a catalyst for the leader to grow or to be enmeshed in crisis. The wound presents the leader with an opportunity to explore and question the actual foundation of her leadership and herself. How a leader responds to being wounded can define her as a leader. The wound, at its best, can lead her back to her own true story.

Behind the Mask

Leadership lives are, for the most part, determined by role expectations. These roles often do not fit with the deeper personal needs of
a leader. In times of crisis, questions of identity and role are usually
heightened and move to the forefront. A wounding experience,
inextricably linked to a leader's role, can serve as a painful reminder
that the very role itself can put a person at odds with his own needs
and identity. A crisis experience, then, is apt to provoke a leader to
ask, "Why can't I be myself and be the leader? If I'm not really being
myself, who am I?"

The leadership role that administrators assume shapes how they
approach their practice, what they are able to accomplish, and how
they think about their work; most important, it also shapes what
they feel and believe the role permits them to feel. Leaders are often
told "Don't get angry," "Don't be wrong," "Don't look weak," "Don't
look like you don't have the answers." Many principals, superintendents, and headmasters that we talked to felt they were defined
and confined by the boundaries of their leadership role. For some,
this meant being faithful to their role but not to themselves.
Although living the role of leader, they found they were out of tune
with their emotions and growing ever less true to themselves. They
also found they were losing their connection to the people they
served. What is it about leadership that makes it difficult for a person to be a person in his leadership?

To be a school leader is to be more than a screen on which the
wishes of others are projected. The stories suggest to us that in a
leader relationship the leader can be overly influenced and defined
by the desires of significant others. If a leader feels he needs to act
out of the wishes of others, considerable ambivalence is experienced.
Nevertheless, parents, teachers, and students do expect to see certain qualities in their leaders and ascribe meaning to the leader's
action or lack of action. How a leader manages this process is, in fact,
a skill of leadership. The ability to preserve a hold on reality, such as

control over the definition of one's public self, is a challenge of leadership, and perhaps also of experience and maturity. If the community's expectations for leadership clash with how the leader perceives the role, the leader may experience self-doubt. Yet even if the community and the leader agree on the role but it does not fit the reality of the school structure and culture (as discussed earlier in this chapter), the leader begins to question herself, her motives, and her own capacity for understanding, controlling, and perhaps leading the flow of events. This seemed to be the case with Bruce, the principal who was falsely accused of changing student athletes' grades and who was wounded at the core of his identity. His mantra became "But that's not who I am." He felt he was not being understood and that he had lost control of how others saw him.

A misfit between the leadership role and one's identity, or between the role and the reality of work life, can diminish a leader's chances of being genuine. To be sure, environment and behavior are always interacting elements. Leaders must bring their personalities to the roles they play. Who they are influences how they play their roles. Most school leaders, including those we interviewed, would admit that the role itself requires a certain amount of method acting, a style obliging a performer (leader) to respond as much to his own inner feelings as the requirements of the role. However, the goal in method acting is dramatic effectiveness, with the emphasis placed on understanding the character. Such a method can lead in some cases to largely undisciplined acting; that's the rub. If a leader goes too far in acting the leadership part, he may begin to lose himself in the process. That is the wound. It is a daily struggle to allow all sides of oneself to be acknowledged; to be whole is especially difficult during a crisis.

The search for identity is not a modern problem. All of us are engaged in the struggle, in one way or another and throughout our whole lives, to discover our identity, the person we are and choose to be. The practice of leadership makes that search public and pervasive, involving role, style, and appearance. At a more personal level, it involves the leader's choice of values and relationship to staff, students, parents, schooling, and society. The literature and media typically tell of heroic leadership. The leader is often cast as larger than life, a Hollywood-type character who is supposed to be the lone hero fixing the crisis and saving the day. This traditional and public perception of leadership has filtered into the culture of the school so much that the community expects and feels entitled to heroic qualities in its administrators.

Most of the individuals we interviewed would consider themselves ordinary leaders. Some would acknowledge they were in the process of becoming more authentic leaders because they used their wounding experience as an opportunity to learn and develop. As in being faced with a serious illness, the leader may use this occasion in her career to peer behind the mask, to question how she can maintain her leadership identity and self-image, and question even if she should.

Inevitability of Wounding

Wounding is an inevitable part of leadership; it might have to be considered part of the job. It seems virtually impossible to avoid wounding; if one chooses such an approach, then that too perhaps is a wound. A secondary school principal put it well: "The non-negotiable that I come back to most often is being true to myself—heeding the call of my heart, my core, for better or worse. Sooner or later, a true leader is going to stir the pot and, if great things happen as a result, is going to get splattered and slopped on. Spillage is inevitable" (Hallowell, 1997, p. 55).

Spillage is inevitable, no matter how much the heart is heeded. Leadership life is a messy business, as most administrators will attest. We have talked to many school leaders and have yet to find one who has not been wounded in one way or another. Each practitioner we invited to participate in our study had a story of wounding to tell; in fact, some leaders needed time to think about which story to share. When we speak to veteran administrators, they too affirm that crisis and wounding are simply part of the leadership realm.

The school-life riptides, mentioned earlier, often thrust leaders into currents that have the potential to take them away from their goals and dreams. External forces and demands infiltrate schools and can have a powerful influence on the career of an administrator. A school leader today, for example, is apt to be experiencing the pressure of budget cuts; overcrowding; shortage of qualified teachers; and a set of local, state, and federal mandates, many of which are unfunded. Harsh realities from the outside, such as poverty, inadequate health care, and unemployment, create enormous challenges for a leader inside the school. Such challenges undoubtedly cause dissonance and can contribute to the crisis that becomes a wounding experience for a leader.

The culture and norms found within schools, discussed previously, present unique challenges for the leader. The ground-floor conditions that we described—including the way time, space, and communication patterns are structured—are integral parts of the messy world of school leadership. An administrator has virtually no time for reflection or talk with trusted colleagues about concerns and fears. Although surrounded by teachers, students, staff, and parents, a leader can easily be isolated and may have to bear the burden of leadership alone. The chronic work-life tensions a leader experiences present him with significant personal obstacles.

Although we say that wounding is inevitable, we recognize that a leader may try to defy the odds. Some individuals believe that for them it will be different; they can avoid getting hurt. A leader may put up barriers, but try as he may, the ebb and flow of political streams, social forces, and human foibles sooner or later lead to wounding. Bruce, whose story we just heard, may have been able to do something differently in his leadership practice that would have averted that particular crisis and wound, yet in time something else would likely have gone awry. That's the nature of schools and leadership. No one is immune.

Leadership wounds may inhabit a leader's far past or present life, or even both. Some leaders vividly described wounding experiences that, as we listened, turned out to have happened decades earlier, yet they spoke as if it were only yesterday. Some leaders said the wound had become a touchstone for them, a way to recall their vulnerability and learning from crisis experiences. Wounds may help to fuse past with present and present with past.

Practicing and aspiring leaders will understand better the complexities of their role if they acknowledge the ever-present possibility of crossing over to the kingdom of the wounded leader (Sontag, 1978). Understanding that wounds are part of the cycle of leadership may make it a little easier for a leader to respond with grace and accept the inevitability of wounding.

A Double-Edged Sword

Leadership is often shaped by the response to what can be seen as inevitable challenges and crises. Of course, leadership life is, in most respects, no different from any kind of life; it must, by nature of the reality and complexity of school life, alternate between the cycles of risk and loss, jubilation and frustration, openness and fear. Leaders therefore respond to these cycles in different ways. How a leader responds can define him or her as a leader. As we said, a wound is a potential catalyst for a leader to grow, or it can enmesh a person in crisis. Indeed, it is a double-edged sword. The surprising thing is still how surprising this truth can be.

Facing a crisis can be a time to focus sharply on what it means to be a leader. Interestingly, the same experience can be perceived as exhilarating to one leader while wounding to another (consider how some school leaders struggle with standardized testing and accountability and others do not). However, a leadership achievement can become a trap in just the same way as a so-called leadership failure. The ambivalent nature of wounding obliges us to differentiate between the necessary wound that serves as a catalyst to the next stage of growth and one that inflicts further injury. A wounding experience reminds the leader that life is shaped by the cycles of success and failure. Yes, even in descent, the wound is the chance to examine a leadership life anew.

Bruce was unable to convince the school board that along with not knowing this was happening he personally disapproved of such unethical practice. Ultimately, he was fired. We witnessed in Bruce a tangle of anger, hate, and determination as he attempted to exact revenge on individuals who he believed were responsible for his demise. Elusively, almost imperceptibly, responsibility for the misdeed—for the culture that allowed this to occur—appeared in his remarks and then quickly disappeared again. When we left Bruce, he was trapped in the raw bitterness of his leadership wound. He could see only one side of this wound's legacy. His wound was deep and infected by the raging bitterness of revenge. In time, he may choose to see it all differently, to meet it with understanding and let it go, trusting that something new will eventually be born for him.

We fully acknowledge that not all school leaders are willing or ready to ask the hard questions and face their shadow. A wounding experience can change people and also remind them how hard it is to change. The meaning of a wound itself can change with time; the sword can be turned. Not surprisingly, we find that leaders talk about their pain differently afterward than while enduring it. Although we frame the response in binary terms, we recognize that a leader's work life and learning are experienced fluidly and dynamically.

The Sacred Call

The wound thus can serve as a call to examine the foundation of one's leadership. Like illness, a leadership wound brings not only difficulty and danger but also awareness and opportunity. For some of the leaders we met who had sacrificed their identity and integrity in the name of leadership, the wound was a wake-up call to their real self. They found the means—some call it courage—to shed inauthentic ways of being and became truer to themselves, more whole again. For others, the change was not about being different, but finding new meaning in what they were already doing. Some leaders used the moment to resist becoming anything else, hoping to move forward into the future unaltered. Some were changed spontaneously and unthinkingly from within or without. Still others were changed deliberately and consciously, never easily, never for sure, and only with effort, insight, and courage. The experience of leadership suffering—of the wound—is itself a defining characteristic of leaders and leadership. It is, in days and in times of crisis, a most perplexing, and at the same time potentially life-changing, search.

2

Anatomy of a Wound
Where Does It Hurt?

Our attempt to define a leadership wound, the purpose of this chapter, places the experience within varied streams of meaning of which it is an integral part, among them the realms of myth, medicine, and above all the person. We recognize the practical and sometimes harsh reality of the wound, but our hope is to encourage people to think about this kind of experience with a feeling of compassion and responsibility. Leaders may then understand their own leadership with a greater sense of meaning, purpose, and identity.

What exactly is a wound? It's hard to say. Is it an illness, an injury, or an event? Is it a disappointment, a problem, a "disorienting" (Mezirow, 1991) dilemma, a crisis? Is it graffiti declaring "the principal sucks!"? Is it a parent or a teacher confronting a principal at a public event? Is it vague suspicion, or outright public condemnation in the press, on account of questionable performance? Is it the ignominy of one's school being publicly singled out as the lowest performer on standards-based achievement tests? Is it physical and emotional exhaustion from being too many things to too many people? Is it feeling as if one's role, personal beliefs, and actions are simply an empty strategy for getting through an administrative day? Is it when the leader acts as though he is something he is not?

These are just some of the story lines we have heard in our conversations with school leaders. The stories are rich and varied; they do not fall neatly into simple categories. All describe painful nerve roots in leadership work. As such, these scenarios present sources, circumstances, and conditions that in some cases lead to wounding. It ultimately depends, as John Dewey said, on the quality of the experience which is had (Dewey, 1963). The wound is best understood where it hurts.

On the surface, wounding draws from the endemic and chronic tension affecting leaders, all leaders—tension, as Evans (1996) argued, that is by no means wholly new; however, the context of schooling today certainly makes the dilemma seem new, more intense, and more real.

Finally, there is what poet John O'Donohue called "the inner face," the whole-hearted soul of a human being, so vital and essential to the spirit of a person's life. The leader's inner face is attempting to achieve a genuine level of engagement with others and with the world through this thing called leadership. It is our guess that the wound reaches down and around these layers, touching them all in one way or another. We have come to believe that amid this bewildering wounding complexity there are two essential questions for the school leader: Who am I, really? How can I be myself in my leadership?

We do not say that leadership wounding defies understanding altogether, or that it cannot be defined; nor do we imply a mystical quality to it. However, we must admit at the outset that the wound, by its nature and in this particular context, ultimately eludes precise theoretical comprehension. We know of no simple conceptual framework or technique that can account fully for the kind of story described in this book. Well-intentioned, reasonable school leaders inevitably find ideas, plans, and actions resisted by others who have their own reasons for doing so. Leaders and leadership conditions therefore may be shaped by the very human and personal response to forms of resistance. Vulnerability of all kinds—as well as clarity, honesty, humility, and humanity—may be called forth in leadership practice. It is these tensions that seem to be most at stake in understanding the wound and the practice of leadership.

So, where does it hurt? We are told it hurts mostly at the heart of leadership, in a person's essential being. It does not hurt that much if people do not like the leader, if a decision is questioned or if a project fails; but we are told it hurts tremendously to have a motive impugned, integrity questioned, and truth denied. Similar to what we saw happen to Bruce, the principal whose story we heard in Chapter One, it hurts when some essential part of oneself is misunderstood, misrepresented, and maligned. It hurts when leaders are not known or understood for what they really are. It hurts when leaders behave in one way while in reality their feelings run the other way.

What is endangered, then, is what is evoked most fundamentally by the work of leadership: a person's integrity, identity, fallibility, and spirit. There are potent conscious and unconscious forces evident in leadership work that have an enormous capacity and thrust toward growth when the opportunity presents itself. However, there are obvious challenges to a leader becoming himself in leadership and for reasons that reside outside and inside the person. To find and be oneself in leadership is to find the patterns, the underlying order in the ceaselessly changing flow of leadership work, and to let those experiences tell the story. The meaning of wounding is imbedded in the realms of mythology and medicine; inevitably, though, leadership wounding points toward issues in the personal realm of vulnerability, isolation, fear, and power. These are elemental and inevitable by-products that become the shadow aspects of leadership work. They form a foundation for our understanding of the wound.

Call to Consciousness: The Mythological

As a universal aspect of human experience, the wound can be elaborated in a number of ways. As a symbol, for example, it has been memorialized for centuries in the crisis stories of myth and legend. In such stories, the crisis is resonant with meaning where problems

and difficulties represent the sacred wound or the call to consciousness through which a person enters a journey.

A classic story of the wound is found in the twelfth-century
myth of the Fisher King, which is a part of the Grail Legend (Johnson, 1993; Jung and Franz, 1970; Weston, 1993). There is an extraordinary and extensive literature to which the Grail Legend has
given birth. Each has widely different elements. There is, however,
general consensus on some aspects of the story and, for our purposes,
they are as follows.

A certain king, known as the Fisher King, is suffering from a
sickness caused by a wound. There are numerous variations on the
precise cause of the king's wound. Many point to an event in his
preleadership (pre-king) days when, as an impetuous prince, he is
walking in the woods and finds a salmon roasting on a spit. Hungry,
impulsive, and tempted by the smell of the salmon, he reaches out
to taste it. It is hot, causing him to burn his fingers and drop it.
When he puts his fingers into his mouth to soothe the burn, he eats
some of the salmon. It is said that he is so wounded that he lies
alone and isolated in agony in his castle for all but the last three
days of his life. (The only thing that assuages his suffering, it is said,
is fishing.) His illness, for mysterious and unexplained reasons, has
a disastrous effect on his kingdom, depriving it of vegetation and
exposing it to the ravages of war.

The king's castle holds a special cup known as the grail. Any
person who drinks from the cup instantly receives what he or she
wishes—everyone except the king, whose wound cannot be healed
by the cup (or anything outside himself). As a number of interpretations of the legend have it, the wounded king can only be restored
to health if a certain knight (named Parsifal) finds the castle and
asks a particular question.

Parsifal sets out on a quest as a young knight. After a complicated journey, he manages to find the castle; however, in his ner-
vousness and confusion, he neglects to ask the question and
everything remains as before. As one interpretation of the legend

goes, Parsifal must spend a great many more years fighting ogres, dragons, and giants; defending castles; and aiding the poor. Later on, closer to midlife, Parsifal ends his long journey by locating the castle once again; this time he is composed and brave enough to ask the king the right question: "Why are you wounded?" The moment Parsifal asks the fateful question, the wounded Fisher King is miraculously restored to health, and the whole kingdom rejoices.

There are a great many interpretations of the Fisher King story. We offer one. The Fisher King is actually named Amfortas, which in French (*enfertez*) means "infirmity"; in the German version it means "he who is without the feeling function" (Johnson, 1993). This may be a useful way to understand the wound. It is the loss of the authentic spirit of the leader, the essential force of a person's nature, the true feeling function.

How do real feelings get lost in modern school leadership? So many of the self-described wounded leaders we have met shared the myriad ways in which they had come to inhabit their roles. Some felt they were "hiding behind their functions," or were "prisoners of roles," or became so identified with work that they had "lost" themselves. The sense of hiding behind a mask, façade, or pretense, whether held consciously or unconsciously, has been well documented in the leadership literature and called the "imposter syndrome" (Kets de Vries, 1993). Indeed, many leaders adopt survival strategies by inhabiting a role and playing a part that imprisons them, moving further away from what they are inwardly experiencing. The effects of this on a school can be devastating, for both the leader and the organization. The king's wound, then, understood as the loss of the feeling function, suggests that his generative capacity to value, give pleasure, and bestow a sense of meaning to life is missing. Perhaps this is the invitation that some have been waiting for: to understand the leadership path as the work of the cool, rational, and precise strategic mind, but also to understand leadership life as a deep expression of the whole person—and to understand what it means to find one's real self.

Some interpretations suggest Amfortas inherited his power without having won it by his own effort (Johnson, 1993). Grabbing at the salmon (symbolizing knowledge and power), the young, inexperienced prince acquires it without the necessary kind of experience that would earn or teach him its use. Many beginning school leaders recognize that they have positional authority and power, but they do not yet possess the personal leadership power required to get things done. Most school leaders must find a way to reckon with the vicissitudes of power inherent in the role—or, for that matter, in any person inhabiting the leadership role and their own tentative relationship to power. How ironic that the wounded Fisher King should find solace in fishing, in searching for the thing (power) that wounded him in the first place. Similarly with a leadership wound, by returning to the source of pain leaders may discover something integral about themselves and their relationship to power.

The Fisher King's wound may be understood as a kind of emotional reckoning, maybe a necessary preparation for another kind of consciousness, signaling a leader's internal willingness to wrestle demons that keep parts of a person hidden from himself and others. Sinclair Lewis's *Babbitt* and William Foot Whyte's *Organization Man* suggest the stereotypes of another age in depicting the leader as missing some essential part of himself or herself. As the story goes, the deepest part of ourselves, as symbolized in the king's wound, can only be healed by the innocent, self-conscious, and instinctive qualities of a Parsifal.

Parsifal, the innocent fool, the figure from the tarot deck, is often described as a spirit in search of experience, arousing an image full of contradiction and paradox. Parsifal seems always to be on a cliff's edge, unaware of the danger. Instead of looking down, he is looking up, unable to have the perspective to see how close to danger he is. Usually, there is a little dog barking at his side (which some interpret to symbolize our animal, instinctual side), which reminds us not to get lost in the clouds. Balancing the temptation to get lost is a cane or stick (the will). He uses the stick to carry his purse (his

knowledge), which is depicted as small and fragile (experience stored in memory). Parsifal seems ready to venture forth, happy and innocent, reminding us of our own sometimes foolish and vulnerable nature, a vulnerability that might save us if we acknowledge it.

Again, the fool is a familiar figure in myth, folklore, literature, and drama, playing an important role in relation to the king. The fool often plays a "transformational role" (Kets de Vries, 1993) as truth sayer. Kets de Vries maintained that within this relationship, the destinies of the leader and the fool become intricately bound in a common fate. The fool creates a certain emotional ambience and through various means reminds the leader of the transience of power. He becomes the guardian of reality, while paradoxically presenting the pursuit of foolish action.

The fool is often represented by the young person, always walking toward the abyss, turning his back to the light, and facing his shadow because the sun is behind him. Perhaps because he doesn't know better, it is said, he mistakes the darkness for the light and sees it as reality. He lives in his imagination, under the "law of accident," without realizing it; he tends to blame life for the events he encounters and for putting him into the situations that his own innocence and foolishness have attracted.

Ironically, Parsifal possesses the very qualities (through his innocence, awkwardness, and vulnerability) necessary to let the king know that he is wounded. These may be the same qualities that the leader must rely upon to see her real self—the innocent fool inside, the spirit of the person who is open to the world because it doesn't know how not to be. The first step to healing depends entirely on knowing that one is wounded. How ironic it is—not toughness or arrogance—that these essential and more awkward traits lead to restoration and growth for the king. It is these qualities that give him the power to see by allowing the one essential question to be asked: Why are you wounded? It is this question that bestows the gift of self-consciousness on the king, the opportunity to see his suffering in a new light. The question itself symbolizes the gift of consciousness and awareness; the meaning of life is not to be found in the quest for power and advancement but in the meaning one can make of one's own life.

"Why am I wounded?" The question that brings the king to consciousness is, of course, the most basic question a leader can ask: Who am I? This question asks the leader to look inward and deeply at his wound and at the life that led to it. The question encourages the leader to get acquainted with what is going on within and to become open to all elements of the leadership experience. Tackling this question is a lifelong process, not some static achievement. The challenge is to be able to stay there in the leadership questions, to inquire further, and to unlock one's leadership: What are the parts of myself as a leader that I fail to know or see? What parts of myself can't I let others see or know? What if all of me showed up?

Call to Consciousness: The Medical

The Fisher King story has its modern equivalent in a remarkable and burgeoning literature of illness narratives. There seems now to be profound recognition of these same themes in daily life and across a variety of contexts. Most notable, for example, is the story of a college professor who decides to "teach" the lessons of his own dying in *Tuesdays with Morrie* (Albom, 1997), a book that was on the *New York Times* bestseller list for more than two hundred weeks. Many of these stories reframe illness-as-enemy to illness-as-teacher, evidenced by the vast testimony in the literature of individuals who have overcome physical challenge and limitation. This literature has continued to inform and inspire our thinking about wounded leaders (see Armstrong and Jenkins, 2000; Bauby, 1997; Cousins, 1979; Diamond, 1998; Frank, 1991; Kleinman, 1988; McCrum, 1998; Post and Robins, 1993; Radner, 1989; Remen, 1996; Sacks, 1998; and Verghese, 1995).

A crisis occurred a few years ago that made these themes very real and close to home. Bob is a close friend, a forty-five-year-old physician in what he thought was excellent health and the prime of his career when he found his way to the hospital emergency room on a hot, muggy summer day with severe chest pains. As he described it, he went very rapidly from doctor to patient—and almost to corpse—in the course of thirty minutes, his "doctor role dropping away fast and something much more essential starting to be revealed" as he proceeded from heart attack to cardiac arrest.

Fortunately, he survived the experience and began telling his friends the story of the event and what it meant to him, through phone calls and e-mail. He described the whole experience as having a "before and after" quality to it, similar to many who face a life-threatening illness; "death," he said, "was more of a concept than a reality" before his heart attack.

In the months following, Bob communicated sporadically by e-mail, phone, and letters. His own description and understanding of his heart attack was growing and evolving as his recovery progressed. We began to hear the story in his story, the story he was starting to tell himself, a story (we eventually discovered) that was an integral part of his own healing process. At first, he described the heart attack in cool, clinical terms, filtered through his physician's training and language. His e-mail descriptions were quite detailed, like the clinical notes a physician would be expected to write to himself after an examination. Soon, however, as he put it, he realized the doctor part of him was no longer "in control" of this event. His story began to change in subtle ways as he came to understand his heart attack differently. He subsequently described his experience as "dying to live," saying, "It comes after we have let go of something, first, of the way we thought things were supposed to be. We all have expectations, a kind of model in our minds of how life should go. My own experience is that much of this is unconscious, but we become aware of it when things stop going our way, when the expectations are not met. And we need to let go. Letting go of what we want, what we thought was going to be, and instead accepting what is. So much easier to say than to do, and it is not a one-time thing, but a process. I do try to apply it to myself, and when I have seen others understand their suffering in this way, true resurrections occur. Not always the physical resurrection that one would have really wanted, the cure, the remission, the restoration of function. But other things. We learn to let go of past grudges, forgive others, forgive ourselves, open ourselves, break out of the self-centeredness that has, unknowingly, trapped us and kept us disconnected in a deep sense. Death has opened my eyes to life, literally."

Another physician, Jerome Groopman, a world-renowned researcher in cancer and AIDS, wrote eloquently about how patients deal with illness (1997). He argued that although there is no universal epiphany, unequivocally each individual experiences some kind of change process, for better or worse. He suggested that sickness holds a range of meaning for people but that isolation and bearing the burden alone just increase pain and suffering. In addition to good medical care, he argued, patients need an outlet to express themselves and to discuss their fears and other emotions. They require tender, careful support in understanding the experience and in navigating the treacherous world of sickness and medicine to help ensure that their change is for the better, whatever the medical outcome.

Groopman further pointed out how "the process of retelling can be one more way that the reality of the situation is accepted" (p. 105). Stories are important even when the ending is unknown, which is often the case with an illness narrative (and with a leadership story). The telling and retelling of one's story is a way to reconstruct a life narrative and find a place for the uninvited illness, or in our case a leadership crisis, in a person's life story. A disruptive illness or leadership crisis can force one to face questions about one's way of leading and the meaning of leading. Questions arise as to the kind of person and leader one has been and is, and how to sustain one's identity in the face of such an event. In this sense, the construction or reconstruction of the life narrative, like Bob's, can represent a kind of moral quest in the hope of assigning the event a place in a person's life narrative and investing it with meaning.

A healthy tendency is to eliminate the taboo around leadership illness and let the ill and wounded tell their stories. Groopman, Frank, and others found that ill people need to tell their stories to reformulate their perception and relationship to the world. We believe the wounded leader shares this need (addressed in Chapter

Eleven) to develop circles of friends, a community of support, people to turn to during the difficult times, people with whom one can ask the questions and have real conversation—in order to transcend the isolating conditions of wounding.

Call to Consciousness: The Personal

Is it possible to be a real human being in leadership? Chris Argyris (1985, 1987) argued that personal development in the workplace is dependent on a certain richness of environmental context that allows people to take risks, experiment, and feel safe enough to display their authentic self. Yet so many conceptions of leadership focus on the external aspects of leadership behavior, emphasizing what the leader should "do" without understanding the inner landscape of leadership—that is, who the leader "is" and how she is brought to consciousness around her own foibles and fallibility. The leadership life, we recognize, is a complex balance of conflicting forces and tensions that manage to function most of the time. The wound is signaled, however, by the opportunity to no longer take things for granted.

There is a need to understand a wound's etiology; why and how did this happen? It is equally useful to study how individuals respond to a wound, to explore coping and healing strategies; this is where we have primarily directed our attention. Although each leader's story has its own special choreography because each person is unique, there are elemental themes of vulnerability, isolation, fear, and power manifested in the wounding experience.

The Vulnerability Paradox

Raymond Callahan coined the concept of the vulnerability thesis in his classic work *Education and the Cult of Efficiency* (1962). He carefully documented how business values and practice had a powerful influence over American public education. What he also learned, to his surprise, "was the extent, not only of the power of the business-industrial groups, but of the strength of the business ideology in the American culture on the one hand and the extreme weakness and vulnerability of schoolmen, especially school administrators, on the other" (pp. vii–viii).

Callahan had not expected to find such diminished professional autonomy; nor did he expect to find how often superintendents made a decision based not on educational principles but on a need to satisfy critics and to hold onto their jobs. He said, "I am now convinced that very much of what has happened in American education since 1900 can be explained on the basis of the extreme vulnerability of our schoolmen to public criticism and pressure and that this vulnerability is built into our pattern of local support and control. . . . The point is that when the schools are being criticized, vulnerable school administrators have to respond. . . . This is an inadequate and inappropriate basis for establishing sound educational policy" (p. viii).

Callahan attributed superintendent vulnerability to how schools were financed, asserting that "so long as schoolmen have a knife poised at their financial jugular vein each year, professional autonomy is impossible" (p. ix). This "vulnerability thesis" has been used by many over the years as a way to explain the high turnover rate of superintendents; it has also been seen as an excuse (by those, for example, who do not accept Callahan's thesis).

Vulnerability persists as a relevant matter in leadership life today. Business continues to be a dominant force in education; in fact, we hear echoes from the Callahan era reverberating through the current school environment. Business leaders and politicians have joined forces in today's educational policy arena to support and argue for their agendas. We find a multitude of new policies, regulations, and legislative reform-based mandates that challenge and haunt school leaders. Public criticism and pressure is centered on school accountability. Many argue that standards-based reform is an equity strategy, and school leaders are being (perhaps rightly) challenged to devise ways to close the achievement gap. When we speak with school administrators, we find that they are indeed asked to be responsible and accountable for resolving these issues, and more. The vulnerability thesis is as relevant today as it was in 1900 (Eisner, 1985; Lutz and Wisener, 1996).

Today, we attempt to avoid any contemporary conclusions about the generic causes of wounds and concomitant issues of who or what to blame for them; instead we move toward exploration of how leaders can understand and use their wounds in the context of their own vulnerability. Vulnerability, as leaders' stories tell, can be a strength, not a weakness. Our emphasis here is on the inner landscape of leadership vulnerability and the sources of wounding that can be understood and determined from the inside out. Indeed, beneath the surface of a leadership wound is a complex and interrelated constellation of key elements, among them vulnerability, fear, power, and isolation. In the words of Carl Rogers: "The very feelings and experiences which have seemed to me most private, most personal and hence most incomprehensible by others, have turned out to be an expression for which there is resonance in other people. It has led me to believe that what is most personal and unique in each one of us is probably the very element which would, if it were shared or expressed, speak most deeply to others" (1961, p. 26). Here's the vulnerability paradox: wounding can be a time of the heart's greatest vulnerability. A school leader may steadfastly avoid the inherent traps and feelings of vulnerability only to awaken and find that in the very opening the wound offers, she may find her real self.

Isolation

It is still, unfortunately, lonely at the top for school leaders. Philip Jackson (1976) described this condition years ago in a personal and poignant essay entitled "Lonely at the Top: Observations on the Genesis of Administrative Isolation." Many school leaders continue to be isolated at the top of what Lucianne Carmichael (1985) called "authority pyramids." Thus it is not surprising that despite emerging emphasis on shared leadership (Donaldson, 2001), teacher leadership (Moller and Katzenmeyer, 1996), and building leadership capacity (Lambert, 1998), the school leader is still prone to feeling alone and isolated, not merely in the physical sense but in a deeper emotional sense too. It is not the kind of isolation born of solitude, even if the organization is structured nonhierarchically. Stress from a curious kind of "public isolation" is a constantly recurring theme in leadership work. Isolation in a fish bowl creates chronic tension and is a paradox for the school leader (Evans, 1996). The interpersonal and intrapersonal elements that contribute to such feelings, we believe, are subtle and form the basis for a profound form of wounding.

Necessary boundaries in leadership life require a degree of administrative isolation relating to personal and professional roles, visibility, decision making ("the buck stops here"), and confidentiality. Many of the leaders we met told us they had gradually learned how to deal with the requirements of their role, deflecting criticism by growing "scar tissue" and "binding" their anxieties in work. As we said before, the chronic tension affecting the leader from without and within has the school leader spending most of the time being other-centered, with success begetting success: "the more you care and the more helpful you are, the longer stretches the line of problems to solve and people to help" (Ackerman, Donaldson, and van der Bogert, 1966, p. 165). Being of service in the school and community can make the school leader a magnet and an object of public sentiment about schooling and a host of other issues, easily threatening the barriers between public and private, career and family, and professional and personal that many need for a sense of balance and meaning in their lives.

Crossing boundaries, however, creates a subtle form of isolation that seems to occur primarily because the leader has lost the right balance in her own belonging: To whom do I belong, to me or them? Many school leaders described their own particular wandering in the conspiracy of busyness and the constantly orbiting planetary cultures that Donaldson (2001) described so well. Many navigate the mine-field out of a circumscribed role, the very role distancing itself slowly from others, as well as from their own feelings, losing themselves in the process.

What does it require to come out from hiding, from behind the insulation and the isolation? How can leaders remain true to their own interior? Is there a common ground from which no leader can be distanced, or isolated, or excluded? If leaders are to be permitted to be whole, these are just some of the challenges confronting them and their schools.

Fear

The leadership life is influenced, and in some cases determined, by fear of one kind or another. Most school leaders, however, like to keep their fears at arm's length, being reluctant to admit, at least in public, that they have them at all. A common fear of the school leader, described in our conversation, is that of not measuring up. This fear is often associated with the traditional cultures of school-ing that place high value on competition, productivity, and achieve-ment at any cost. The challenge for many school leaders to remain afloat in their position as principal or superintendent is not neces-sarily to overcome their fear; it is to know *what* to fear. As we see in the stories that follow, the wound creates an extraordinary context for seeing and understanding the specific nature of leadership fears. As such, it is simultaneously the place where the leader needs to look more carefully and courageously, and the very place that most fills the leader with fear.

Leadership fear takes various guises: fear of appearing weak, fear of failure, fear of change and of not changing, and fear of being judged and criticized. Many administrators have an understandable fear of being fired—or worse, of losing their career identity. Prac-titioners who have reached the higher echelons of organizational life typically have invested a great deal of themselves in their careers to get where they are; consequently, personal identity is intertwined with the leadership role. The threat of losing that position, of being told they are not good enough, can be overwhelming, even devastating. Such fear can engulf people, sometimes temporarily, other times permanently. Fear is a potent emotion; it can erect barriers that separate the leader from the school community. The leader can easily become trapped in a negative cycle of fear and isolation.

Paradoxically, fear can also work to one's advantage. If constructive, fear can be a gift. Sending signals that there is danger, it propels people into action; some people may even find courage through fear. A universal fear of educators is (or should be) that they will fail to educate students and thereby break their covenant with the public. This reminds us that if fear is managed well, it can be positive; it has the potential to spur people on to do what is needed, what is right. One key is to find the balance between too little and too much fear; another is to realize that the equation varies with the leader.

Perhaps the most challenging fear of all is that of really showing up for leadership. To be fully present, passionate, and committed in a real and personal way with all of one's fears and desires in tow is among the greatest challenges of leadership life. In his classic book *The Wounded Healer*, Henry Nouwen said, "Nobody can offer leadership to anyone unless he makes his presence known—that is, unless he steps forward out of anonymity and apathy of his milieu and makes the possibility of fellowship visible" (1990, p. 65).

The irony, of course, is that a school operates as if such fear does not exist; the culture of the school and the culture of leadership do not offer much solace. We expect our leaders to be fearless, and most leaders also believe that they ought not to be afraid. It is a reckless expectation. Fear is part of the human condition of leadership and schooling—particularly when wounded—and needs to be acknowledged, accepted, and (we daresay) even embraced.

What would it mean to be fully visible as a leader? In the principal preparation classes that we have been teaching for years, the experience that many students anticipate with greatest dread is the act of public speaking: the first faculty meeting or student assembly. This is not surprising. It is often hard to hear or hide from our own voices speaking in those times. What would it mean to face the life of leadership on and off the stage without such fear?

Power

Leaders rarely feel they have real power. The paradox of power leaves leaders aware of their vulnerability and their dependency on others. Put simply, most school leaders are surprised at how little real power they have.

The leaders we talked to all had positional power. They were vested with formal authority in their position as principal, headmaster, or superintendent; some were discovering just how tentative their power really was. The school leader is traditionally given tremendous responsibility, but not a lot of authority. Vulnerability helps remind the leader how elusive power is, regardless of the job title.

Power usually finds its inverted face in fear of powerlessness (McClelland, 1975). Power is a central force in schools and in the lives of school leaders, driving them as well as wounding them and others. Power, strength, and competency are traditionally sought after as important qualities in leadership. Balanced use of power is critical to school life, creating common goals and giving meaning to work. A school functions through power structures of one kind or another. Pervasive and predominant conceptions of power in our culture and schools define it in terms of the ability to control and impose one's will on others. Yet power is essential to a leader's success in leading change and realizing goals. Consequently, power has traditionally gone hand in hand with leadership and played a major role (as does fear) for good or bad. Failure to recognize the many faces of power, that it can be used constructively and destructively, forms a foundation for wounding.

The community expects the leader to act quickly and to exert power. We have seen that a leader must tap an enormous amount of energy to hold back and not rush in to be the fixer. It is a powerful act of leadership to wait, listen, and not solve the public problem, but rather serve to support the community in owning the problem and struggling to confront it collectively. This requires the patience to wait and the willingness to take time for a process to work. This goes against the norm.

Most of the leaders depicted in this book wrestle with the ambiguity of power in their own leadership. Concern about power permeates the stories, regardless of the context of the wounding experience. Two central questions emerge: How do leaders come out of the shadows of their own fears to discover the elemental nature of their power? How is leadership power empowering for school leaders and for others?

Ironic Blessing

The wound can ultimately be understood for what it is: an opening in the body, a place made vulnerable to injury, infection, and perhaps change. It is, as David Whyte says, "the very place we are open to the world, whether we like it or not" (2001, p. 129). In our view, the deepest obligation a leader has is to engage continuously in a reflective process of making sense of his leadership, and trusting his influence on others and on the school. For many leaders we have been fortunate to meet, including a number you'll discover in the stories that follow, their trust in the integrity and vitality of their own leadership is inevitably balanced and shaped by their shadows—creeping self-doubt, fears, and questions. Many say it is primarily these aspects that keep them honest and on course.

Personal change inevitably runs up against entrenched forces and is experienced as difficult, forced, unnatural, and sustainable only through considerable effort and will. Therein lies the possibility for an awkward, though perhaps more courageous, vulnerability that invites others into the conversation rather than keeps them out. The leader doesn't have to have all the answers, doesn't have to be ruled by fear and driven by displays of power, and doesn't have to wound others and himself or herself in a mutually wounding cycle that is ultimately self-sealing and isolating. This kind of leadership welcomes wounding not as a burden but hopefully as an ironic blessing.

Part II

Wounded Leaders

"Ahhh, I know someone who . . ." When we tell a colleague or a group of educators about our work with wounded leaders, the response is often similar to when one tells the story of a battle with a life-threatening illness. The story strikes an emotional chord. Like illness narratives, everyone has had a comparable experience, knows someone who has, or recognizes that this could happen to him or her too. Perhaps these stories resonate so strongly because they remind us that anyone's life can be interrupted at any moment by sudden illness, or in this case, by a crisis in the workplace.

The stories in Part Two represent a sampling of the kinds of crisis stories that wounded school leaders have told us. The seven stories beginning with Chapter Three illustrate how leaders approach their wounding and their interpretation of what it means to them. We have taken great care to use the words of the leaders and to construct each story as they have done for us. Although some of the practitioners granted us permission to use real names and places, others were understandably reluctant. Therefore pseudonyms are used in all the stories, and we disguised distinguishing features to ensure confidentiality.

In the annals of leadership cases, these stories are hardly extraordinary. Their everyday quality is precisely what makes them worth telling, for each story describes in its own way how an administrator grapples with a leadership crisis. The stories chosen represent wounding experiences that have taken place in diverse socioeconomic settings, in a number of regions of the country; they vary in terms of school and district level. Some stories tell of a recent experience, while others tell about something that happened years ago, offering insight into how leaders may come to understand their wounds differently over time. The precipitating event for the leader's wound ranges widely, involving everything from a full-scale district crisis to progressive problems; we are reminded that a wound can occur in any context.

The first story, "Great Expectations," in Chapter Three, is about how a leader's life can easily be determined by role expectation. It tells of leadership betrayal, thwarted ambition, and deceit. This is the story of an individual we call Mike, who enters his first superintendency and must choose between upholding a court order to desegregate schools and the wishes of school board members to ignore the judge.

The second story, "Fragile Power," has to do with power and fear of helplessness, central forces that drive many school leaders and at the same time wound them, as well as others. This is an all-too-familiar story of a principal, Sandra, who is conflicted by her inability to prevent a student from entering a life of crime and her lack of power to eradicate student violence.

A contemporary story of high-stakes testing and how this leads to the wounding of Alice, a dedicated principal, is featured in Chapter Five, "Branded." The story reveals that despite heroic efforts to improve test scores, if they don't rise fast enough the principal is shunned and stigmatized by colleagues. We witness a leader striving not to be subsumed by the role.

In Chapter Six, "When the Bubble Bursts," we present the story of Sharon, a principal who is exhilarated about the prospect of crafting her vision of quality education in a brand-new school that she was selected to open, only to discover she has become the scapegoat for a disgruntled, antagonistic, and divided faculty. In this story, we see a leader who struggles to accept her vulnerability and trust her intuition.

Carlos's story, as told in "Trapped in a Cocoon," is striking because at first glance it seems so familiar. This is the story of a new principal faced with the dilemma of either remaining true to personal beliefs about leadership or else changing to gain the trust of teachers. It is also about coming to terms with the possibility that a perceived strength is weakness.

In Chapter Eight, "The Trial," the wounding experience is embedded in a success story. It is about a principal, Nancy, who believes she is supposed to be selfless, self-sufficient, and tough. She learns these are the very qualities that can prevent her from listening to her own needs.

In Chapter Nine, "Dancing on the Skillet" tells of Christopher, a superintendent who reached what he thought was the apex of his career only to find that upon a change of membership on the school board he is about to crash. This story reveals the tension a leader experiences when, conflicted by a powerful desire to keep his beloved position, the demands to please others clash with his leadership style and values. We see him try to balance who he genuinely is with his own expectations and others'.

Our intention in telling these stories leans toward a holistic view of leadership life—specifically, what it means to be a wounded leader. We have tried hard not to separate who the leaders are from what they do, think, and feel; thus we do not portray them as a series of disembodied experiences. Equally important, we seek to avoid having the reader experience them as disembodied persons. Our hope in each story is to render the person visible and hence understandable by emphasizing his or her relationship to the things thought, felt, and done, and the wound. We've tried to tell these stories in such a way that the reader will come to understand who these leaders are and what wounding meant to them.

All of these stories, in their own ways, reflect an endemic characteristic of leadership and wound: far too often leadership roles do not sustain, validate, or resonate with the personal needs of the one becoming a leader. This, we believe, represents the ultimate wound—the distance a person in leadership travels from his or her own true story.

3

Great Expectations

We were pleased that Mike agreed to meet for an interview. He has a lifetime of experience in education, having served as superintendent of an affluent suburban community and two of the nation's largest urban districts—the "big league," as he called it. The experience Mike chose to relate represented a stormy period in American history, when the civil rights movement brought racial and cultural discrimination to the forefront. It was an era of political upheaval and unrest, a time when people of color pressed for change in the schools to bring them closer to realizing the American dream. This was when the federal courts imposed a desegregation order on his school district. It was also when he discovered that many hidden contradictions, inconsistency, and hypocrisy had infiltrated the world of education.

As Mike told his story, he easily glided across those time periods of his long, distinguished career. It was hard to confine him. He juxtaposed how he approached his third superintendency with the first: "When I arrived in Riverside, I said I'll be there probably three or four years before I get run out of town. Everybody laughed, but that's exactly what happened. I didn't make that prediction in Waterford because it was my first superintendency and I was fresh out of the doctoral program in college and thought, 'Well, by golly I know just about everything you need to know.'"

He told us why he was hired in Waterford: "I knew the city because I lived in it and grew up in it. I knew the school board, which was one of the primary reasons that I was selected as superintendent. The ultimate inside candidate. And again, I thought that I was selected for that position because I had the skill and the ability and the school board in my interview saw that. Quite the contrary. I was naïve and I was theoretically innocent in the sense of being superintendent.

"In other words, I would not have answered the questions in my interview today the way I answered them back then. 'How do people get promoted?' 'On merit.' I believed that. I don't believe that today. I know better. But when I said 'on merit,' the school board thought, *This is good,* and I thought, *These guys are square.* But they knew that wasn't how it was done in Waterford. Highly political. But that's the answer they wanted to hear, because if someone was naïve enough to believe that and not know the difference and not respond as I would today—

"Like when I went to another district here, a board member came in and we went one-on-one without the tape. He said, 'Now, do you want this job?' And I said, 'Well, that's why I'm here.' And he said, 'Well, there are certain things you're going to have to do; for example, we want all twelve central office administrators fired within three months of the time you get here. Are you willing to do that?' I said, 'Of course not. I'm not going to do that because that's not how I operate. If after three months I determine all twelve are a bunch of thugs and no good, sure I'll fire them. But it will be my decision.' 'Well, if you don't do what we want, you're not going to get the job. Goodbye.'

"Now, again, if I were the new, innocent, first-job type I might have thought about that. Or said, 'Yeah, I'll do that.'"

So when entering his first superintendency, Mike was instantly launched into the center of a political quagmire, at a time when the community was divided over the desegregation plan. He was promoted from director of curriculum; there, he said he had been "in charge of curriculum for the whole city and running around doing good work in the schools, working with teachers and kids and loving every minute. It was the best job I ever had. But not aware of the politics in the school board setting, I was very naïve. I had a doctorate . . . and nobody really told me anything about the nastiness." Filled with big ideas and plans for important change, he eagerly embraced his new role as district leader.

The politics of desegregation dominated his life. One critical incident in this context arose with his staff. During this time, he came to realize that "somebody was leaking to the board what was going on. Now, the problem with that was, I had a board telling me not to carry out the court order, and I had a judge telling me to carry out the court order. I had raised my hand to carry out the law, and if I didn't want to do that, I would resign. My idea was I was going to try to get the job done and go around the obstacles. One of the obstacles was the school board."

To stop the leak, he decided, together with one trusted colleague, "to plant a phony story and run it around the tent and see where it comes back." The traitor turned out to be an assistant superintendent he had personally hired, a man twenty years his senior who had been principal when he was a teacher, someone he had respected.

"And so I called him to my office and we sat just like you and I, and I said, 'John, I have reason to believe that you are going out and reporting what's going on at our meetings to Joe Blow. Well, why?'

" 'You,' he answered. 'They gave you the job. I spent thirty years in this school system clawing my way to the top, and then they hand you the job because you went to an Ivy League school. Look at you. Who do you think you are?'

"He gets out of his chair, takes off his jacket, and starts to come at me, and I said, 'John, I'm just coming off twelve years of coaching football, basketball, baseball.' (I was forty years old). I said, 'John, I'm in a hell of a lot better shape than you are. Don't do this, 'cause I'll clobber you. Now sit down.' And 'Aaaah!' He's still in a rage, screaming at me. So much so that one of my aides came in and one of my secretaries came in, and they were scared to death and said, 'What should we do?' I said, 'It's OK, It's OK.' So he's calming down and he's red, and I said, 'You know, John, if you keep this up you're going to have a heart attack.' Now, I said that sort of the way you might say that to me if I was exploding. Within four days, his wife called me at five in the morning. He had died in bed with a heart attack.

"I didn't tell this story to anyone other than two of my top aides, and at the wake I go over to a school board member who is standing in the corner surrounded by a group of cronies, smoking a big cigar, which he used to do at the school board meeting and blow smoke in my face when he didn't agree with what I said. And I said to him, 'Ted, I found out that John was spying on me.' He says, 'Yeah, so what?' And I said, 'How did you get him to do that?' And he said, 'You know, Mike, that's what I like about you—you're stupid. We promised him your job.' I said, 'You promised him the job?' And he said, 'Sure.' 'You mean you would have given him the job?' He said, 'Of course not. If he'd stab you in the back, he'd stab us in the back. But it was useful.'"

Looking back on this incident, Mike commented, "But, you know, that's how you learn stuff sometimes"—the stuff of dirty politics. As disappointments and problems were ground into him, he learned the limitations of people and systems.

When he reflected on this painful time in his career, he identified the major trials encountered along his path to self-realization: "Family stress was the first thing, and then the second thing for me was learning the cynicism of politics." You might say he was descending into the belly of the whale. The desegregation crisis became all-consuming; it even affected his sleeping and eating.

He continued: "The crisis was difficult on me as a person, but most certainly on my family. I have often wanted to do a study on the percentage of divorces of the major league superintendents—very high, higher than the superintendent profession as a whole.

Some people have absolutely no way of relating to what 'the large city group' goes through—no way."

Mike reported, "The problems that occurred strained my marriage, which we managed to overcome, but we had some tough times with that. For example, I had a cop escort me to work every day for a year. Second, we had a police cruiser outside the house twenty-four hours a day for a year. My wife was threatened with rape, sodomy, and all of the above for a year. She received telephone calls from people saying, 'We're going to kidnap your children and we're going to do this to them and we're going to do that to them.' And we had to change the telephone number three different times and it got out three different times, which led me to conclude very quickly that the guys from the telephone company were giving my number out—that is, the residents of the city who work for the telephone company and were opposed to the court order were letting my number out. So, you know, there was that kind of stuff that went on."

We asked him if this experience changed him. He contended, "Oh, undoubtedly it did. It made me tougher and it made me more realistic, more understanding of politics and learning how you have to go around the system. You have to learn to deal with the media, and it comes down to a situation of trust. You can't trust really any of them—the politicians and the media are not trustworthy from the administrative point of view."

Referring to the many hypocrites he met, he added: "You have to be careful not to tinge your life with them. As an administrator you say, 'Now, these guys aren't interested in what's best for the children, but what's best for themselves. Now, how do I deal with that? As an administrator, how do I get things done?' And what it comes down to is a professional trade-off. And I have to think about the ethics of all of that."

As Mike felt more and more out of touch with himself as leader and distanced from the board and their followers, he began to doubt his leadership ability. This was the beginning of his wound. The politics of fear and greed were rampant and infiltrated not only his office but, more significantly, his inner world. His ideals were tested. There was a definite disparity between values and the situation at hand as he listened to board members publicly trumpet their commitment to do what's best for all children and then turn to him and insist that he not carry out the court order to desegregate schools.

As Mike's story suggests, leadership lives are often ruled by society's image of the role. People expect their leaders to behave in a certain way. The community counts on its school leaders to have high standards and do the right thing for students. People expect the leader to fix their problems. Mike agreed with all this, but fixing the problem was not so simple. Indeed, he was not able to fix the problem for this city. He was caught in a clash between the expectations that he and the community shared for leadership and the reality of what was possible.

Mike's experience became an invitation to reconceptualize his thinking about what it meant to be a leader. How realistic was it that he should know the answer? What was it possible for him to accomplish in a short time? A leader can easily become trapped by expectations, society's as well as his own. When his brief tenure ended, Mike left with a new understanding of how people can attribute to their leader's hopelessly unrealistic expectations, and that leaders such as he often share these beliefs. A consequence of believing in such myths is that the leader must eventually fail. If a leader doesn't solve problems and do so quickly, as happened in this story with school desegregation, the community can blame the administrator and remove him from office. People then turn to the next leader to remedy the situation. If that person doesn't miraculously fix the problem, the cycle persists as the community moves on to yet another leader.

Rather than continue to accept the popular mythology about leaders and see himself as a failure, this leader began to change. "And the concept of what the job is, when you go into it you're trying to help children, do what's best for the kids. . . . So you become realistic and you realize that there are only certain things that you can accomplish over a limited period of time—a stewardship that's three or four years in the big leagues. And what can I do in that period of time? What can I do to move the schools ahead a little bit? Knowing full well that your successor will come in and change much of what you're trying to do, not because he or she wants to change what you did, but she wants to put her own agenda forward. So the question is, if you leave the district, what's still there five to ten years later? What is left in the district, anything there that you did, that you feel advanced the needs of children?"

His awakening was acknowledging his vulnerability and limitations as a leader, "because we all can come in with these grandiose ideas." Although he had the courage to oppose the board, he realized that at this time in his career he did not yet have the capacity to challenge the norms or change a stubborn board and its staunch supporters. He had been operating under the myth of leader-as-fixer; now he started to rethink his role as leader.

He also came to know the darker side of school politics and would not allow himself to succumb to that world. The board members thought they could manipulate him, get him to run the district their way, but that was not the case. He said it was something of an eye opener to see in action, contrary to popular belief, that not all educators are guided by what is best for children. This awareness helped to clarify his own sense of purpose and mission.

Despite constant distress and rancor, Mike did not conclude that he was a failure; nor did he walk away from schools over the conflict. Rather, this experience signified a coming of age. The journey of his first superintendency brought both loss and gift—a loss of innocence, and a gift of possibility. With his eyes opened to the vulnerability inherent in school leadership and the reality of school politics, he used the crisis to learn about himself and to reframe the leader role. Unwilling to accept the status quo, he heeded the call for a new kind of leadership awareness and behavior and moved on to another superintendency—a little wiser, and ready to meet the challenge to share what he had learned.

4

Fragile Power

This story was told to us by a successful principal, a veteran of twenty years. Boasting a reputation as a tough-minded leader; consistent in her approach to colleagues, staff, parents, and students; and equally passionate in her advocacy for them, Sandra had been principal of Peterson Elementary for thirteen years. Peterson is a K–8 elementary school with approximately seven hundred children. Most people would acknowledge that "you just don't mess with Sandra."

Sure of herself, she spoke plainly and always said what was on her mind. She didn't hedge: "I work very hard and I play very hard, and I expect others to do the same." Sandra's story surprised us, in part, because she wasted little time getting to what she thought of as her wound. As she put it, "Something has shaken me to the core"; it had to do with a particular student who had been in her school since kindergarten.

She told a story about a troubled boy who was increasingly getting into discipline problems at school, as well as a number of serious incidents outside—theft and harassment of other children while in possession of a weapon. As a result of a court order, the boy spent the summer in a Department of Youth Services detention camp, but by the time school opened in September he was "gang-affiliated," in Sandra's words, meaning he had joined a street gang. This was unprecedented for children at Peterson Elementary. Sandra said she had lots of conversations with him, his mother, the courts, and the school system; nevertheless, she felt the school hadn't had any impact on the boy, who was now twelve years old. When he was caught fighting, he was suspended. But since he had a younger brother at the school, he was responsible for picking him up; then Sandra discovered he was assaulting children outside the building. Two students came forward, telling her they didn't feel safe in the school or on the streets, that the boy and another gang member were stealing their clothing and demanding that they buy them back. They said they were bringing this to Sandra's attention because these other boys had weapons. Finally, Sandra called the police and the boys were arrested.

This is what Sandra first said: "What this left me with, when all this was done and over, was the helplessness of how I cannot protect the students in the school. One of my jobs is to ensure their safety. My students are supposed to be safe once they walk in the door, and I just can't say that anymore. I know that I'm not able to see and know everything that goes on, but you would think that I would have some information, or even an inkling that this young man who has been involved in so many other issues was harassing our kids. And I guess I didn't want to believe it because it was just too painful to think that he was taking advantage of kids to the point that they did not feel safe and were afraid to bring his name up because he is a gang member.

"I felt so helpless on Friday, I went home crying, saying, 'What is my job? What am I here for?' If I can't do the basics and assure that our kids are protected while they are in the school building, how can I do anything else? Because if kids are worried about their own safety when they walk out the door, how can you expect them to want to learn in the school? And how can they trust the adults to keep them safe? Me, being one of them!!! It was a very helpless feeling, to the point that I began to wonder over the weekend if this is where I want to be. I know that I have a passion for what I do, but we're getting into things that are way over my head.

"I do not have—I don't know if the word is *expertise*, but I just don't have the answer. It's a feeling of helplessness that I can't protect these students. And my question over the weekend to the superintendent was, 'What do I say to the parents on Monday?' Here they are, having an expectation for principals—we go through this routine of locking doors, visitors need to check in at the office, we need to know who is in the building, and now I have to protect my kids from my own kids? Two students came to disclose this, and I had no inkling what was happening. And the other thing that was more disturbing was that these children say it's been going on for a month—and I had no knowledge of it!

"To me, the whole issue is about one of the basic roles of principals: about ensuring safety for kids so that they can go on about their business of learning. The question that I keep asking myself is, *What is it I really do?* I don't have the tools to ensure safety for my kids 100 percent of the time, and people will say, 'You can't be everything to everybody; you can only do the best that you can.' But that's not enough, it really is not enough—because if I was a parent in a school where I knew this was going on, I would want some answers.

"So I went home Friday, and I tell you, I wished there was a way I could retire and continue supporting other principals with the work that they do but not be so involved in it. It's not just that I'm involved with these kids—it's my life! And these are my kids! I'm very committed to them, and if I can't keep them safe at the basic level, I don't know what I'm doing. That was very scary for me. I've never felt that way before. It shook me to the core. It really did.

"The notion of helplessness for me as an administrator leaves me paralyzed. And it can be in any arena. It can be around domestic violence, and there's not much you can do about it. When children come to you, you want to be able to make their life right, and yet you know you can't control what happens outside of the school. This is something that entered my school—and I can't do anything about it. What is sacred? And then you have the public out there, and the superintendent, saying, 'How are you ensuring that everybody is safe in that school?' And I'd have to say I couldn't do it. Does that make me weaker as a principal? Does that mean I honestly didn't have tools? I was able to do some stuff; I was able to take the element—the dangerous disruptive element—out of the school; but I can't control what happens out there. Yet it comes back because they are my students, so it's a vicious cycle. Where do principals draw the line? We own it all. I own it when kids get on the bus, until they arrive home—for a student to get assaulted down the street and he's not yet home—he's still mine."

What is the nature of Sandra's wound? At one level, it is about how principals deal with the limits and constraints of their own power and influence. For Sandra, and for many principals today, the issue of safety and its opposite—school violence—is of paramount importance. Many of us remember the principal on the cover of *Time* with a Louisville Slugger and bullhorn, an image that evoked for many principals a number of associations, among them the principal as protector and defender of hearth and home. As Sandra said, "I thought I was protecting our students because I made a big case in the courts and in the school system that this child was not only a danger to himself but he was a danger to the rest of the community here at Peterson Elementary. So having him leave, I thought, was one way to exercise power. But I did not understand that his hand was so far-reaching. He was going to wait three blocks away to shake them down. Kids are now upset and looking for different routes to go home so that they don't run into these boys—they're not even safe in the school, in the neighborhood, in the city."

Sandra's lament raises questions: Where does a principal's influence ultimately lie? Where does it end? For many principals, like Sandra, this is a vexing dilemma, one that has no simple answer. A principal from New York City once half-seriously described the "grounds" of her school as extending through the entire borough of Manhattan. Many principals experience a similar dilemma in defining the zone where their influence ends and that of another "protector"—

a parent, sibling, or guardian—begins. Sandra said: "I've dealt with so many issues with kids, and yet this hit home to me. It certainly gives you a lot of food for thought in terms of what you are doing, your mission, your core, and what is your primary job of being a principal. Certainly, student achievement is my number one goal in the school, and I'm creating a climate where people can learn and be happy, but there's the basics: if you don't have safety, how can you do all the other stuff?"

Sandra was beginning to realize in a vivid way the limitations of her position and power. In her words, "So, hopefully, I learn something from this experience. I know I have. It's something I just can't shake off. There are lots of things I can shake off at the end of the day and say, 'Well, I looked at it, and maybe I could have done it differently, but it wasn't that bad.' I can shake it off. But this really stuck with me! How do you look at a parent who says, 'Can you ensure that this is a safe place for my child?' and introspectively look at that question and finally say, 'No, I can't. I can't promise you that.'?"

A principal cannot promise to eliminate all violence. But she could promise and dedicate herself to working with the community so they can all do their best to stop it, which is what this principal eventually did.

Nothing frightens school leaders as much as feeling helpless and impotent. Whatever the reality of the circumstances, the *feeling* of helplessness is a source of deep wounding. School communities, for their part, are equally unforgiving in these domains. Excusing a lack of achievement based on circumstances out of their control brings little solace to school leaders who believe they are supposed to be in control. The highest irony is that solving the immediate problem rarely brings the healing that is ultimately necessary. Sandra was able to remove the violence from inside her school, but it only moved around the corner, and that was still not good enough.

Yet because many school leaders are unaware of what fragile power they have accumulated, they can scarcely admit to themselves or others how much powerlessness and helplessness, or fear of help-lessness, influences them. Productivity, achievement, and winning are traditional measures of leadership and the leader. Impotence, powerlessness, and helplessness in all their forms are worse than death for most school leaders.

Sandra's wound (in contrast to Mike's, in Chapter Three) was still fresh and raw when we met her. The source of wounding for leaders like Sandra is the inheritance of a world in which a leader's value is to defend something that a leader, acting alone, cannot defend. To be sure, defender of the school may be an honorable role, but it is a role at best and not reflective of the whole person. Simply put, principals cannot do it all; to begin the process of healing, they must first risk the painful realization that they can't.

When we left Sandra, she was recommitted to leading the school and had only begun to heal. With some distance from this crisis and time for reflection, the challenge for Sandra is to use her learning from this experience and integrate it into who she is as school leader.

5

Branded

J ust a short drive from some of the wealthiest communities in the state and country, Martin Luther King Elementary sits in the middle of one of those depressed areas that America's economic boom passed by. Economic, racial, and political barriers divide this community from its neighbors in rich, gated enclaves with superior schools to such a degree that we see few similarities between students. This may be why so many people were shocked when Alice actually volunteered to transfer to Martin Luther King after she heard the principal there had had enough and was taking early retirement.

Alice traded a comfortable position as principal of a school where children were doing fine on the state-mandated achievement tests to take the helm of a school with the distinction of being on the state's dreaded list for critically low performance. This bold move brought in tandem the thrill of helping kids who many thought were doomed to fail and the grief of becoming a wounded leader.

When she approached her boss about applying for this new opening, she told us, "His eyes got as big as golf balls. He started jumping up and down. He's saying, 'Oh, my goodness, I have done something right in my life. The Lord has answered my prayers. Because I really wanted someone to go to Martin Luther King who wanted to be there, who wants to work with this community. That believes in this community.' I said, 'I am that person.'"

Alice was returning to the community where she had been born and raised. Unlike so many others from her childhood, somehow she had not succumbed to pervasive despair and instead went on to become a teacher; in fact, her first teaching job was at Martin Luther King Elementary. She knew even then that she "wanted to be in a position where I could help make decisions for the children. I knew I had to leave and then come back one day." So she served as administrator in other schools until she returned home to assume her third principalship. Although her family supported the change, many of her colleagues were puzzled. She told us, "At meetings, when it was announced I was going to Martin Luther King, I started getting all these stares. And people were coming up to me saying, 'Ahh, what's the situation?' At first I couldn't understand, and then I started to feel it." Some were suspicious and asked, "Well, did you do something wrong? Why would you leave that school to go to Martin Luther King?"

School opened in the fall. Alice immediately began to get parents involved. She believes that parents of the children in her impoverished urban school want the same things that parents in the upscale suburbs want, including a good education. She also was keenly aware that the school would never get off the critically low-performing list, with all its negative repercussions, without the support of parents. At a faculty meeting, she asserted that "working in a community like this one, you have to get the parents involved because I don't care what kind of curriculum you have, I don't care what programs you have; if the parents aren't involved with it or if education is not important to them, it's not going to mean anything to the kids." Thus she began a major crusade to include parents in the education of their children. Building such relationships was a hallmark of her leadership.

In reaching out to parents, she was simultaneously trying to persuade the entire community to begin believing in its elementary school again. She said to teachers, " 'OK now, what we need to do is to get the community involved. Let them know that this is not just a building over here with 98 percent of kids eating free or reduced-cost breakfast and lunch out of taxpayers' dollars, and teachers who aren't doing anything.' I just told them how people thought about them and this school. The thinking is people do absolutely nothing over here. They think that teachers don't care about the kids, care really nothing about the parents, and absolutely nothing about the community. I said the only way this can be changed is if we change it."

Now a tradition, one preplanning day in the fall is held at the community center, with teachers and community members, including a core of retired teachers who still live in the neighborhood. She exhibited tremendous empathy with the community.

Alice embarked on a public relations campaign to get "our new story out there." Parents were invited to come to school to find out about the tests that were constantly featured in the news. For 50 percent of students, English was a second language, so arrangements were made to have translators available and material was sent home in multiple languages. A march was organized to announce to the town the importance of the testing and to show how hard everyone was working to prepare for the high-stakes tests. Students, parents, teachers, business partners, church leaders, elected officials, and other community leaders all participated in the event. Alice excitedly told us, "There must have been two to three hundred people gathered here that Saturday morning. We started the march at school, went up Main Street, through the neighborhoods where the majority of our kids live, and we ended up at the community center." That got people to pay attention. Suddenly, she had people asking, "What can we do for you?"

Seizing the moment, she elicited the help of volunteers to tutor and read to children. "One church," she told us as an example, "asked, 'How many fourth graders do you have?' [Fourth grade is one of the years in which children must take the state-standardized tests linked to promotion and accountability.] I said, 'A hundred and twenty.' The minister said, 'I'm going to get you 120 volunteers.' He didn't get the 120, but he got pretty close to it, and those people were coming in here all year doing one-to-one tutoring with our students." Alice knew that test scores had to go up, so she opened her school at seven in the morning for before-school tutorials; she added, "We pulled kids during the day, we had after-school tutorials. The focus was on raising those scores."

She also told people, "We are going to need supplies because the thing was that students would get referrals because they didn't have a pencil or they didn't have paper." Eager to halt this practice, she said, "We got boxes and decorated them and took them to every church in the community and said, 'Please bring in supplies.' The first year, they did it. The second year, it was like a competition to see who gathered the most supplies." Clothing and shoes were also donated, and the principal reported, "If a child comes to school with tattered clothes on, it's my job to go find something that looks a little better." Alice believes that she has to do everything she can so that a child is ready to enter the classroom and learn.

Tapping the school's business partner for a grant, she opened up her school until 6:00 P.M. a few days a week so that students could stay to do homework and study. With the money to staff this program, children were able to have access to computers, books, encyclopedias—"the things they need to do well." With this grant she was able to fund a series of evening meetings for parents about how to help their children with school and to reinforce the importance of doing well on the state's standardized tests. Dinner and babysitting services were provided. She also found funding to continue the practice of translating all forms in multiple languages, "so that when a report card comes home, when a progress report comes home, parents are going to know how to ask for help."

In addition to parents, she knew she had to convince teachers to believe in themselves again and to believe in the children, to empathize with them. Teacher-parent conferences were revived, but she told us, "I sat in on a few conferences and a couple of times I wanted to crawl under the table from embarrassment." She would not tolerate a child being humiliated. The tone of meetings was recast to be professional. However, "it started running around that the teachers get no support when they are in meetings with parents. An anonymous letter came out of this situation, sent to my supervisor. I addressed it at a meeting: 'When you are right, I am going to be with you. You need to be careful what you say to these students; these kids are human beings too.'"

Tensions arose between the principal and teachers over discipline policy. At a meeting, one teacher recommended that "when the students misbehave what we can do is take them to a room and darken all the windows and make it real smelly and put dirty stuff, garbage, in there. And make 'em stay in there all day." Alice might have exploded at such outrageous comments but did not. Instead, she turned it around to make a point. She told us: "People were applauding. Then I stood there and said, 'OK, I will do that under one condition. Every time you do something wrong, like not turning in your plan book on time, coming late to work, not teaching in the classroom when you should be teaching, when you have kids missing the bus, not scheduling conferences with parents that you should—if I can put *you* in there, then I will agree to do the same with students.'"

She added, "'You don't have to love these kids, but you better darn sure pretend that you love 'em from the time they get here in the morning to the time they leave in the afternoon.' So at the end of that year, more and more people started transferring."

Since then, she has been able to hire some teachers who match the school's new philosophy and values. She cautions them, "If you come here, you are going to have to work hard." She was crystal clear about her own beliefs and feelings.

That first year Alice was principal at Martin Luther King, she announced: "We need a quick fix to get off that list. You know, sometimes you have to promise kids something. I want all of the fourth graders to go to a theme park." Again, she recognized the emotional needs of children, their need to feel good, their need for rewards.

To her delight, a business partner came up with the money; more important, the kids earned the trip by reaching the school's goal for the tests. But four years later, the problem, she says, is that "consistently our scores for the last four years have gone up, but we always come up just short." Why? "Because they raise the bar. So here comes that F, which is really devastating." The scores required for a school to stay off state and district lists for low performance keep changing, keep getting higher; yet she has no voice in state policy.

Her words shaking with emotion, Alice says that her school always falls just below the new requirement and consequently remains in the negative spotlight, despite test scores increasing each year she has been there. Her frustration is palpable. Unrealistic targets and the fear of failure have caused other principals to escape to less-threatening settings.

Achieving test scores acceptable to the state, let alone an A, has proven to be as elusive as the Holy Grail. Alice shared a touching story of how, the night before her maiden voyage with standardized testing at Martin Luther King School, sleep was postponed. Up with the day's first light, she drove to see her brother, a minister. "It's about five o'clock in the morning, and here I am knocking on his door. He says to me, 'What are you doing over here so early in the morning?' And I went in and said, "I'm sorry. Let's just pray. If it means anything, pray over these pencils that the kids are going to use to take their tests today."

Notwithstanding her extraordinary efforts, this principal reported that people are constantly pointing fingers at her for low performance. She felt stigmatized. In her words: "It's always on your mind. When you go to meetings, there's talk about F schools. You are getting looks . . . it's almost like wearing the scarlet letter." Visibly upset, Alice continued: "Sometimes I would be sitting at the table with my colleagues, and there would be laughter towards people who are at the F schools. It was devastating; it was hard." There was talk at the district meetings that anyone who worked at an F school would get a cut in pay. Once, she attended a school board meeting where she and the other leaders of F schools had to sit in the front row to be lectured. A board member admonished the group that "if scores don't go up, we will reconstitute your schools." Alice commented, "We each walked out of there with our head down. That was devastating, to be on TV with the whole world watching." She felt vindicated the next day, when another board member called to apologize personally for what happened and said, "I feel bad that I did not speak out." Alice expressed that she needs a stroke sometimes, like everyone, and wisely stated: "This crisis is not an Alice thing; it's a school district thing. I can't take the blame myself." It seems that the state and district focus on a test score masks the poverty that plays a big part in causing it, instead placing blame on schools, parents, kids, and principals such as Alice.

Other times, she would have to listen to administrators at meetings worry aloud about how too much money and extra resources were going to the F schools, which meant that their schools were losing out. They spoke of their fear of becoming an F school because of places like Martin Luther King that were siphoning an unfair share of resources. Still other times, she would meet exclusively with the handful of principals in her district whose schools had been graded F, which was very emotional too, but at least some comfort.

What confirmed for Alice the branding as principal of a low-performing school is the evaluation she has received from her supervisor every year since arriving at Martin Luther King. As principal, she can be rated "below, at, or above expectations." She says, "That hurts me a lot, because there are portions of your evaluation that have to do with your testing. As hard as we work, I have yet to receive 'above expectation.' I get so upset sometimes I will have to call someone and say, 'Pray for me, I am going for my evaluation today.' I am sitting there and my mind is on nothing this person is saying, until they flip to the back page. And I see 'at expectation,' and I say, 'Why?' As hard as I work . . . and the scores have consistently gone up for four years. I mean, these scores are higher than ever before. Our math went from 23 percent to 58 percent, tremendous gains. I am a strong person, [but] I tell you, I cried all the way home."

In tune with her emotions, she anticipates how she will feel when she goes for her evaluation. Displaying emotional self-management, after sitting through yet another disappointing evaluation from the district she experiences anger and then calls "two or three people to get it out of the way. Then I start to laugh about it, like, whatever. You have to go through that emotional part of it."

She confided in us that "it was like testing had just consumed my life. I would come home and I would be talking about it all the time." One year, there was a fiasco with the test administration; a teacher gave the wrong directions, children scored poorly, and it meant the school earned a failing grade. Exasperated, the principal said, "I thought I was just gonna chew 'em up and spit 'em out. I was just that upset. You know, we worked so hard. It was like I was almost turning into a monster over this test, because I never yell at people. I don't go at things that way. I could see it was really having an emotional effect on me. I got so defensive. It was just a killer inside."

The demands of Alice's job are enormous; she told us that "people think I'm a superwoman. I'm supposed to be strong. Children come to me with problems other principals couldn't imagine. You know, I am that one with all of the world on my shoulders saying to teachers and parents, 'Come to me if you have a problem and let's talk about it.' It was like I had everybody's problems on my shoulders, every test." One night, Alice went home depressed about the test and called her brother. He counseled her: "Like I told you before, do the best you can every day. And when you leave school, you know that you've done the best you can. Step away from it, and be the wife that you need to be to your husband and the mother that you need to be to your children."

Not unlike her community, Alice feels shunned and branded. Similar to Sandra's (Chapter Four), her wound was recently acquired and stinging. Yet unlike Sandra's crisis, which was sparked by the actions of a juvenile delinquent, Alice's crisis appeared to be growing bit by bit as she tried to move her faculty and increase standardized test scores. Her wound has led her to doubt her role and question, "Why am I doing this? Why am I here?"

We asked her how she copes with the stress of this job and the pain of being stigmatized. We wondered what motivates her to keep trying after so many setbacks. She said that one way is to surround herself with positive people and to talk things over with her family. Similar to her goal of making the school a sanctuary for children, she tries to create her own private sanctuary with family. As her husband reminded her, "You said you wanted to be the light of this community, and that's why you're here." It helped her to assert that "I know I'm going to stay here and start all over again." Her enthusiasm and persistence supersede failure.

Alice seeks understanding and comfort by listening "to my inner voice and writing poetry. Poetry helps me to hear my inner voice. Sometimes I allow my feelings to come out in the form of a poem." In addition, a deep spirituality sustains this leader. God's presence in her life offers light in the darkness of despair and helps her to believe "I know there will be greater rewards for me somewhere." She said she is "still learning to divide my time to be able to give my family quality time, time for here at work and to have time to reflect. . . . I won't tell anybody it has been easy." Faith and optimism help to keep Alice from becoming overwhelmed.

Some would say the world has turned its back on Martin Luther King Elementary School and Alice, but she is able to reframe the negative and find the positive. She is fighting for the children in her school and fighting to prevent her leadership wound from becoming fatal. She told us about a dream she had. She was at the state capital to address the governor: "The governor stood and made an apology to me about the letter F assigned to our school. He said, 'I don't look at F as failing. The F was supposed to mean Fighting Forward to a Fantastic Future.'"

Alice has discovered that "when I go through things it makes me a little stronger, it makes me a little tougher." She is a survivor of this community and living a labor of love. Learning from her wound while experiencing the pain and beauty of her community only adds to her faith and determination to change this school "and make it shine."

Through this story, we are reminded how leaders, even those who are truly strong and tough, can be hurt by leadership. Branded principal of an F school, Alice was abandoned by colleagues and others in the community—including, she thought, the state government. She could easily have lost her way. Yet she didn't. She never lost sight of her mission to organize teachers, staff, and community to improve the education of children at her school.

The challenge for this principal is to keep looking for ways to separate the role from the person. She must continue to learn through the trials of leading. She was living the role of leader who had the weight of the world on her shoulders, but she also had the wherewithal to tend to personal needs. Rather than joining the silent conspiracy to deny the emotional side of leadership, Alice not only focused on trying to solve education problems but acknowledged the immense emotion that accompanies her life as principal of an oppressed school. She struggled not to take the blame for a situation she inherited, even though she felt penalized, and she also worked at not blaming others. Instead, she harnessed her emotions and leadership strategies to move the school forward as best she could.

6

When the Bubble Bursts

When we first met Sharon, there was an air of excitement in town. A new school was opening and the school board had recently chosen her, an experienced administrator with a fine reputation, to be principal. Little did she know that she was about to enter the most trying time of her professional life.

Sharon was thrilled; it was her dream to start a new school, select her own staff, and realize her vision of quality secondary education. But the summer before school began, the bubble was already bursting. She told us, "Well, when it came down to actually being able to select the staff, that did not happen. I ended up hiring seven teachers out of forty-one. The rest were all assigned to me." Initially, she was delighted to learn that fifteen teachers from one site had volunteered to move to her school.

"I thought that was great, until I found out how the fifteen people volunteered. The principal called them into the office and said, 'If you stay here, you will be put on documentation and I will work to get you out of the system.' So that's how I got my fifteen people. The seven people from another school were marginal, and again, they weren't told that in so many words, but they knew that the writing was on the wall. So I started right off the bat with twenty-two people who wanted to be here, but they had an ax to grind. And then I brought seven people with me, so I had really three main groups of people. I had the kind of incompetents who were not too terribly upset about being here, the fifteen who did not want to be here, and they were going to prove that they were going to do what they wanted to do and the principal was not the boss, because there were fifteen of them. And the seven I brought were looked upon as being the chosen few because they were my people."

The rest of the teachers were surplused from local schools. "Well," Sharon told us, "this is what I started with. And I mean, I have never had a problem working with staff before. I've always prided myself on being a team player. I can be a leader and I can be dictatorial, and I can do a lot of other things, but I've always believed in shared decision making, and I've always gotten along very well with my staff and we do a lot of problem solving together. That's what I thought I was going to be coming into. Needless to say, it was a horrendous first year." Acknowledging that most teachers had arrived with mistrust of all administration and unwillingness to take ownership of anything, teachers thrust a lot on her, and she admitted that she allowed it to happen.

Sharon told us how, although good things did happen that year, there was much "back-stabbing and one-upmanship." The staff was divided into groups that did not get along: "So, I had no cohesion. It was a cauldron; it was horrible. And then on top of that, one of the teachers who was an isolate was such a poor teacher that I had to start proceedings against her for termination."

When looking back on the debut year of her school, Sharon talked about how she tried "to get these people blended together, to get them to trust me." As she reported it, "That first year—and I never had a grievance filed in the prior thirteen years as a principal— I had nine grievances filed against me. And none of the grievances ever came to me first; none of them followed the contract. They went right from the teacher to the union, from the union to the district. So, I was battling that. It was really rough."

As Sharon relived that year for us, she explained how she began to doubt herself: "It was a year when I really started to question my abilities of being a true leader because I looked upon it as my failure—

that here I've brought people together, and even though they came with all this different baggage, it still was my job to make it cohesive, and to fix it. It was very frustrating. I never anticipated that this would happen. I was always the peacemaker. I've always had good relationships with people. And it just hit me right between the eyes. I mean, I was shocked."

Sharon went on to say, "Basically, I am comfortable with my knowledge and my ability to do things and make things successful. And I think I have an uncanny ability to see a lot of different solutions to problems, and I can feel comfortable with almost any of them. And so in a shared decision-making model, I don't feel like I have the only answer. But when I was really being—what I felt— backed into a corner, when these grievances were coming at me, I wasn't willing to trust the process. I was afraid that the decisions might be, 'Well, let's get back at her,' or 'We think this will backfire, so let's do it.' And I don't know if that was true, but that was my perception."

Agitated, Sharon recognized that she was afraid and worried but wasn't sure what to do about it; her past experience in this instance did not immediately suggest an appropriate response. Her fears became counterproductive. She felt isolated and vulnerable.

As she questioned her ability to do the job, she found that suddenly she needed the authority of her title, "because that's the only thing I knew to fall back on. So I needed people to follow what I put down in writing, or what I wanted them to do. All of a sudden, I didn't want anybody else's input. It was my power, and it was almost like, 'This is the only thing I can do.' I became helpless. The power wins out when you become helpless. When you make a directive, that's power." Sharon suspended shared decision making and relied more on the autocratic side of leadership. She asserted her values and beliefs about schooling and let people know how disappointed and upset she felt.

Sharon was fighting to survive. In her words, "When you are in the midst of turmoil and uncertainty, not knowing what you need to do, you question yourself continuously." She feared she was becoming weak. She told us that at no time, however, was defeat an option. She had to address the fear and figure out a way to meet this challenge.

During this time of intense vulnerability, Sharon experienced the isolation that often comes with wounding. Asked if she felt alone, she responded, "I really did. You don't dare let the district office know you're not successful. I have two principals who are really good friends, and I would just call and say, 'What do I do now?' And sometimes it was even, 'Don't tell me anything to do; just listen to me.' Because you can't really share anything with anybody in the school. As much as I could trust—and I have some very good friends on staff—there's always that line of demarcation, and I would never put a friend who is a teacher in the position of being my confidant. That would be unfair. It was a very stressful year."

Sharon was wise to seek support in the right places so that she did not lose control of her emotions and act in ways she might later regret.

Never giving up hope, she embraced this crisis. Over time, she began to trust her intuition again, and the fear of being weak dissipated. In hindsight, she said, "Maybe my gut feelings were the right feelings because I am not sure that I could have come out of the situation as positively as I did without going with those gut feelings." She also came to realize that it is appropriate for a principal to articulate her values about teaching and learning. In addition, she learned that it's OK to show her feelings about what she sees happening and that it is important to pay attention to what feels right. Knowing one's emotions and how to manage them is a leadership asset.

Two and a half years later, Sharon reported, "We still have some of the same problems. A couple of people have left. One is out because I terminated her contract. A couple of people have turned around and realized that I'm not the horrible person that they thought I was going to be. We do a lot of trust-building, team-building activities. The people who were the most negative are still on staff and pretty much my negative people today. But I think that I've been able to understand them well enough that I can capitalize on their strengths and give them some power. And I think that's what they're looking for: control over their destiny."

Sharon has reached out to her faculty to try to better understand their perspective and show compassion for an individual's situation. For example, she now acknowledges their need for autonomy.

Most principals we know believe they must show strength and dread the thought of being labeled a weak leader. This is what their community expects of them. Yet principals do sometimes feel vulnerable, often hiding their vulnerability from others and even themselves. But how can they grow and develop as individuals and as leaders if they must always conceal or deny their fears? Sharon did not know how to accept her vulnerability at first and began to doubt her own ability to lead—distancing herself from her true feelings and the leadership role she'd assumed.

With her personal power threatened, her intuition led her to rely on positional power. She found the behavior worrisome because it did not fit with her theory of leadership. Yet this gut feeling or emotional wisdom steered her away from a disastrous course. Showing strength and being in control without displaying anger became, for a time, more important than practicing her preferred (and perhaps unidimensional) style of participatory leadership.

She perceived this as a weakness. Yet it may be that a direct, more authoritarian approach was appropriate for a brief time. Consider how the school was in a state of disequilibrium. Most teachers did not want to be there; the faculty was divided into warring factions, and the principal was a scapegoat. It was a culture that existed in embryo; the organization did not yet have shared values, norms of collaboration, or an accepted plan for conflict resolution. People were stressed.

Sharon, we suggest, was right in following her intuition and restoring order. She recognized what was really happening, as opposed to what she wished. People had been distracted from the real issues and problems of the school. She needed everyone's attention so that they could begin to trust each other and get ready to do the hard adaptive work of creating a professional learning community and collectively developing an effective program for students and families.

First, by using the power of her position, she mobilized people. Second, by communicating her fears for the future success of the school, she had in effect set off an emergency alarm system among faculty. Third, by eventually empathizing with the teachers, she began to connect with them. These three steps were crucial to her success as a school leader. Looking back, she says, "Maybe that was the best leadership for that given time. And by doing that, I think people then saw where my true beliefs were, and even though I had to dictatorially tell them this is what I believe and this is how we are going to do it, I think it allowed them to clarify for themselves, 'Well, this is what this lady is really about, and this is what she believes. Maybe the way that she is getting us to buy into it is not appropriate, but at least we know where she stands.' And I think that has made a lot of difference."

Four years after the opening of the school, Sharon reported that they are "gelling as a staff," speak a "common language," and are talking about core values. The school has experimented with team structures, and teachers are enthusiastic about becoming a learning community. From an external-accountability perspective, the students are performing above average on the state's mandated standardized tests.

Fear was replaced with the courage to change in the uncertain terrain of leadership practice. She adapted her leadership style and risked exposing her personal vulnerability to her colleagues. As it turns out, her strong emotions about the crisis echoed those of some staff members and served to awaken others to the need for change.

Reflecting on this crisis, Sharon asserted that she definitely is better off because of it. "If you would have said, 'Can I take this away from you?' while I was in the midst of it, I would have said, 'Absolutely.' But now I think, in hindsight, there was a reason for it. I'm not glad it happened, but it's OK that it happened. I definitely think I'm a better person. It's taught me tolerance; it's taught me patience. It certainly has made me go out and look for other skills that I didn't have in my repertoire . . . negotiation . . . reading people. It's given me a lot better ability to find the humor in things that happen. When everything seemed to be crashing down, I had to search for something to bring me back up, have a good laugh, and then we're off and running again."

Perhaps laughter is the best medicine! "It's coming, but it's been very slow," she said. Then, summing up: "It's been very difficult. And it's been an ego deflator for me too. I think I'm a little more realistic now. I really think I'm a better person because of it, and probably a better leader."

The challenge for this principal was to use her leadership wound to learn about herself, to face her fears, and to change. In her story, we saw that, over time, she was able to assume responsibility for her own well-being while getting better at responding to the needs of teachers and staff. She began to accept that she does not have to appear invulnerable and that it's OK to listen to her intuition. Understanding change in herself was essential because the essence of what leaders do is lead change. As leaders change their own lives, they are better equipped to appreciate what it means to help create the conditions for others to change their lives.

7

Trapped in a Cocoon

When Carlos was appointed principal of a large suburban elementary school six years ago, the district office informed him that there was going to be major restructuring. This meant many of his staff would have to be transferred at the end of that year, and in the years to follow.

Thinking about entering his first principalship, he told us, "One of the things I swore that I would do is that when I had information, anything that I was able to share, I would share as soon as I could; information is power." Carlos also spoke at length about his belief that "building relationships and building trust is perhaps the most important thing that I can do in order to shape the culture of the school." So that's exactly what he set out to do. As a result, he demonstrated some understanding of the importance of handling relationships and the interpersonal side of leadership. Despite such positive assertions, the culture he expected to create was not yet within his grasp. Instead, a novice principal found himself increasingly isolated from teachers in his building and mired in strained relationships. He was someone with a strong concept of the kind of leader he wanted to be and the role he would play, but unwittingly he did so at the expense of many people around him.

As he relived that difficult time, he related how "we started the school improvement process very early so that we could be visioning all year. 'What are we doing now? What do we hope for the future?'" At the October faculty meeting, he said, "I started to talk about what we're going to begin to look like next year." That's when he chose to share the power: "I made a public statement that we would probably be somewhere between ten to fifteen fewer faculty members the following school year because there are programs that are going to be relocated." In retrospect, he admitted he had not anticipated how faculty would feel; his misreading of these feelings made it difficult to invite and make safe the sharing of opinions and feelings about job reassignments.

From Carlos's perspective, he was simply "sharing information. No one could ever say that there was anything covert. As soon as I knew for sure that it was in writing—I shared that and the fact that no one was going to lose a job—we're all going to work—that no one was without a home." Needless to say, the news was not well received.

In retrospect, he noted that he "didn't realize, when you looked at Maslow's hierarchy, that really shook their foundation. Even though everyone understood that they were going to work the following year, teachers attach themselves to their schools very differently than I guess the way I attach myself to the district." He recognized he had misunderstood their needs, imposing his own need to know; in effect, he had shut out alternative ways of viewing the situation.

A few days after his controversial announcement, the situation worsened when a group of teachers attended a meeting off campus and confronted a representative of the district office, saying "'Carlos said that we're going to lose ten to fifteen teachers next year. Is that true?' And her reaction was, 'Oh my gosh, he told you that? I can't believe he said that.'" Carlos continued: "So, Linda didn't say yes, she didn't say no, and then she escaped. And she called me right away: 'I can't believe you told them that, you should have waited until April or May when we go to the excess processing, then you wouldn't have to deal with it all school year. You're going to have people upset all year.'"

Carlos reported, "What ended up happening was the group of people that stood around and watched Linda's reaction came back to school and never approached me. But they went among themselves and repeated Linda's response. And they translated that as, 'It can't happen; he's doing this because he wants his own people to be here, and he's looking to trample on half of us.'

"And my feeling at that point was, I needed to maintain my own integrity. I've always lived by the philosophy that you don't react to the grapevine. And part of that is I'll deal with it directly if you come in and you talk to me. But if you don't come in and you don't talk to me, I can talk to you on campus and ask you how things are going, and visit your classroom, but if you don't bring that up as an issue, I've only heard it through the grapevine. And it was real. I do know that that was real. Because a few people did come in, and told me, 'Well, this is what people are saying,' and I said, 'That's not true; it's really unfortunate.' And I even said I understood that Linda said she was shocked that I told anybody. It just boggled my mind that somebody construed that as, 'He told us a lie.'"

Carlos told us how hurt he felt: "I've always worked on being honest with people, and it hurts personally to have people question your integrity, questioning 'Is that information correct?' I don't know if you ever completely get over that, the doubt. And I know that it isn't forever; I think it tends to be that [way for] the first year you're in a new place."

What we see is his attempt to manage his own ambivalent feelings about this process. It seems that this need to run a smooth ship and be in control blocked his own self-awareness, such that he misread emotions in faculty; for some leaders the need to feel essential or be in control can make listening for emotional cues difficult. Likewise, his practicing theory of leadership did not allow room to test assumptions and thereby shut out alternative ways of leading.

Carlos reported that "It was just a very lonely feeling to know that people are upset, and it doesn't matter very much what you say." He stressed that although surrounded by people, the principalship is "a lonely position, and I don't think that everyone realizes that."

Tensions multiplied exponentially as teachers organized an employee building council, "which is a contract-driven teacher group," to meet with him. "So then I have this very adversarial group of seven people that met once a month and the underlying, at least looking back now, the underlying piece that I see that went through it was, 'Well, can we trust him? We don't trust him because he didn't tell us the truth in October.' And that's a really tough thing." Again, we see that Carlos did not yet have the skills to mediate misunderstanding with this group. "It was draining. I guess it was personally draining to not be trusted. I just didn't understand."

We see him striving toward more self-awareness here, recognizing and acknowledging his feelings and pain, but still not knowing how to break out of the situation. He did not accept his negative emotions. Nor was he engulfed by them; however, he was struggling to cope. He assured us that he was being honest and open with his faculty. He thought that by sharing information, he was sharing power. Yet this plan backfired. Negative feelings, tensions, and divisions permeated the entire school year. However, at no point, he told us, did he accept defeat. He believed that somehow he would find a way to work things out at his school. Clearly, he was motivated to change.

Things changed in May. According to Carlos: "Then I dealt with it right up front, when we actually had identified the excess. And I don't even know how to explain it and put it in words right. When I brought that budget to the budget committee and they saw in black and white that fourteen positions were gone, they didn't know what to say. It was almost redeeming for me in the sense that people had walked around saying, 'He lied,' and this is what happened. So, finally in May, I actually dealt with it [with the] full faculty."

After all the fall assignments were made and end-of-year evaluations completed, Carlos stood before the faculty and presented his story. He said: "I apologize. I don't know that I did the right thing. If I hurt people's feelings, then I'm really sorry. I always thought that I should—whenever I had information—that the best thing to do was to share it with people who might get affected therein. And maybe I was wrong. I told you at the beginning that I don't deal with the grapevine. And you've all, I hope, come to realize that my door is open and that you can come in and talk to me and I'll deal directly, but I don't deal with rumors." He had begun to reach out, show empathy, and assume some responsibility for what faculty were experiencing.

Carlos chose a metaphor to describe his wound: "You know that every caterpillar will become a butterfly, and your goal is to get every caterpillar that you're working with to become a butterfly—and then sometimes, as principal, you're stuck with the metamorphosis. Kind of stuck in that cocoon. Because they want to be butterflies but they don't want you to be one; that's how I felt. So I really do believe that a lot of this is about helping the caterpillars get everything that they need to sustain themselves while they're in a cocoon, so that they can break out and fly. But it feels like, in this position, like you're always in the cocoon, and that they don't want you to fly."

His use of this metaphor exemplifies his dawning openness to self-awareness.

He seems to be a sincere person, a man with soaring talent who genuinely wants to do good things for kids and for his school, so it's easy to feel his frustration of being held back. He asked us to "imagine being in a butterfly garden. The whole faculty is in the butterfly garden, and the goal is to get all of the caterpillars to become butterflies. And they don't even want you to come out of the cocoon to fly around the garden. That's kind of how I felt." Maybe he was close to becoming engulfed by emotion; he felt trapped and did not know how to get what he needed from teachers.

Carlos's metaphor offers a vivid image of how he perceived his own wound. He was the outsider. He also felt locked in to one way of being a leader, with no foreseeable exit. As the metaphor aptly says, he became segregated from a large portion of the faculty and was unable to flourish. He wasn't getting what he needed from teachers. From his perspective, the painful insularity he encountered as principal was imposed by a group of teachers; they didn't want him to be as effective as he wanted to be, and this impeded his ability to lead. This interpretation hints at blaming others for what happened. An alternative interpretation, however, may be that he got himself trapped in the cocoon with a little help from societal norms. He became a spectator imprisoned in a drama of his own creation. We suggest another way to understand this wound is to refocus on his "goal to get every caterpillar that you're working with to become a butterfly." His belief about a leader's role restrains his mind-set and gets closer to the source of wounding.

We implicitly, and sometimes explicitly, expect our leaders to solve all of our problems and be responsible for everything. This is not new. In Shakespeare's *Henry V*, right before the battle of Agincourt, the king reflects on how his people look to him for everything: "Upon the King!" he says, "let us our lives, our souls, our debts, our careful wives, our children, and our sins lay on the King!" (Act IV, Scene I). As in the past, we may be making impossible demands on our lionized chiefs.

Rather than developing an interdependent relationship, this principal assumed responsibility, as so many do, for everyone's growth. He alone made the decision that teachers deserved advance information about future job assignments. He imposed the rule not to respond to the grapevine, even when a few teachers approached him about the problem. He clearly saw it as his job to get teachers "to become butterflies and fly." Yet if held too tightly, like a butterfly teachers (and administrators) may be crushed. Leaders need to know when to hold on and when to let go.

Carlos's isolation and inability to break it seems to be an example of how not to manage emotion; by remaining isolated, he only added to his troubles. He would remain distressed, upset, and worried until this changed. He did not, however, get angry; nor did he express rage at the teachers or district. He was able to bounce back at the end of the school year.

He told us that he "walked into the second year as a different principal," and now six years later he can say, "I am a different principal today," implying that his personal change and growth have continued. By way of example, he showed us a "school improvement rubric" that teachers in his school have worked on for the past six months. In his first year as principal, he would have been director of the project; today he's a facilitator. As he lessened his grip on the teachers, they started assuming responsibility for their learning around curriculum. He believes that there is now greater likelihood that the needed changes will be implemented. He has tried to create a culture that expects teachers to be responsible for this kind of work.

When asked how he approaches sharing information with teachers today, he said he has found a way to honor his values yet not stir people up unnecessarily. His current thinking is to share information early on when teachers can have input, a chance to make a difference in the decision or policy. Although some educators will disagree with this approach, he waits to share information if it is a matter over which teachers have no say or control, and if it is likely to interfere with teaching and learning. Regarding the grapevine, he still does not respond directly, but he listens differently, and more. Equally important for long-term survival, he established a strong network of trusted colleagues he can turn to for support.

In order to test assumptions, a leader must acknowledge that he may be mistaken. To do so, he would have to be able to notice the link between his behavior and other people's—an early sign of empathy. He would have to consider that others must be prepared, if he is, to change. Although Carlos is not looking to make mistakes, he told us that he will risk mistakes to move the school forward and be a better leader. He has the ability to believe in himself and learn from mistakes.

The challenge for Carlos is to continue to use his leadership journey as one of self-discovery. His first principalship brought about greater understanding of himself, including learning that some of what he thought were strengths were weaknesses. It also taught him that he must read people's feelings and concerns, and then think about what this means for the school. He now more actively uses these data to initiate and facilitate the work of teachers and staff, so the story is also about learning to understand others' individual needs that may not be the same as his own.

Carlos commented: "I guess the most profound thing about being principal, about being a leader in the school, in the role that I have is that I keep learning more about myself, and there are things that I still am grappling with understanding. I think I've grown a lot. I guess that's why I said this has been more about my learning than it's been about everybody else's. I'm a very different person than I was before this started. I've learned a lot about me. . . . I think that I do the job differently than I did when I started six years ago."

8

The Trial

During the five years Nancy was principal, Chelsea Middle School had undergone dramatic change. The school she inherited had a terrible reputation for failure and violence, regularly finding itself featured in the newspaper and evening news owing to fights, gangs, and guns. It was a place known for abysmally low test scores and a high turnover of staff. Today, however, in middle school circles people often suggest visiting Nancy's school as a paradigm to learn about cutting-edge leadership and innovation.

She enthusiastically told us how hard she and her community have worked to improve the school. The curriculum has been radically changed, the governance system is restructured, teachers have started to teach in new ways, and the school has reached out to parents and gotten them involved. The building received a facelift, technology is now integrated everywhere, and the halls are safe. Presently, their school culture reflects a philosophy of caring and personalization. Attendance is up and suspensions are down. That's why, Nancy explained, she and her staff decided to go for the gold: to compete for a prestigious national award of excellence. They are elated at actually having won the award; "magically for us, it happened." Yet surprisingly, this is what led to her leadership wound.

Nancy told us how she was thrilled because the school achieved so much, but she was amazed at feeling devastated when the district did not recognize the school or her personally. "I feel like we were ignored. The superintendent didn't even call me. A school board member did call, so that does represent the superintendent, but nobody from my part of the district, none of my direct supervisors, called to say 'Hey, congratulations' or 'Well done.' Because we are a school that truly worked hard for it and truly earned it. And I can tell you that our district let us down. By the time someone finally called, it was, like, 'So what?' I mean, it's sad. The excitement didn't carry over as it should have. [laughter] I'm getting over it slowly, but very slowly!"

When asked what she had expected, she answered, "I guess we wanted to see balloons—not really, but . . . I just feel like the system forgot us. I don't know why, because they have honored other schools before."

Nancy was quick to add that the immediate community did rally and show sincere support for the middle school's achievement. The district, however, did nothing until months after the announcement, at which time the principal was recognized at a school board meeting—an afterthought, from her point of view.

Still stinging a year later, Nancy talked at length about how the school gets plenty of attention from the media and district office when something goes wrong: "Then they're all here." Yet "when it's something good, we could not get them."

Brimming with the knowledge of the award, she had looked forward to her annual evaluation. The disappointment deepened, however, when—"I'll be honest with you," she said—"I went for my evaluation last spring. Our test scores had not reached the level they should. The district said that all schools should be at a certain place, you know, way up there." It felt like turning the knife in her wound. "Even though we've made this tremendous progress, my evaluation was going to be average, just average, and it hurt me. What would it have taken to get their approval? I mean, I achieved the highest award you can get. But I felt like I had to beg for a fair evaluation. And I shouldn't have; I should've been able to walk into my evaluation and feel good." Although the national award recognizes schools that excel in academic leadership, the message Nancy got from the district was that her leadership and her school's accomplishments were not good enough for her supervisors.

Nancy reported that "teacher morale has been low this year," despite standardized test scores creeping up. "We can't put our finger on it," she reflected, "because it's not just, 'OK, well, this or that person didn't support me.' And they did to a certain level, but I guess we expected more. It's kind of like you always have these fantasy dreams, and if that fantasy dream doesn't come true, you're disappointed, and yet you may have reached a certain level of it. And I think that's just what happened. Recognition for us should have been the least of what we cared about."

The principal continued: "So I think that's the hurt—that we did so well, we had accomplished so much, and then nothing. I guess at this point I feel like I don't need the praise; I don't need people telling me how good I am. I have my own support group, my own leadership that I can look towards." She reiterated how outside recognition is not what matters. But then she realized that this was not truly how she felt: "Internally, I achieved what I wanted to achieve, but still I felt let down when I didn't get that outside recognition. I guess we always want that mommy's-recognition-type thing."

The lack of recognition from her superiors is a tiny but striking example of a larger problem of unmet needs—of administrators today who have greater responsibilities and fewer resources for support. She did not receive the recognition that she deserved—more significant, the recognition that she didn't even know she needed. She fell into the trap of thinking this should not bother her, but as her story shows, it did. A year later, she is still visibly upset by the experience.

There are many leaders like her who are quick to share their successes with others and are generous with praise, but how is their basic need for acknowledgment being met? Like Nancy, some leaders say that they do not require external approval, that it is enough to know that they are doing well or doing the right thing. They go about their work tending to others and ignoring their own needs. After all, we expect our leaders to be selfless. A leader is not supposed to be needy. Yet when leaders are willing to listen to their own needs, in this case the need for recognition, only then can they begin to respond and heal themselves. Recognizing life's needs is a first step for the leader who wants to flourish. This doesn't mean that he will always get what he needs from others, but by paying attention to needs he can start to replenish and take better care of himself.

When asked how she ministers to her own needs, Nancy told us, "I involve myself with groups of people who are positive. Positive and futuristic educators. I think that's real important because I am always looking beyond. By talking to other people and getting people to say I am behind you, this is great, this makes me feel good. I like a little pat on the back." Nancy also gets valuable support from a group of local principals who meet regularly: "We talk and share with each other. We commiserate, and I think that is the best support."

Another key ingredient in mending is students: "The main thing is that whenever I feel like things are not going my way, I go out and talk to the children, and you know what? They make me feel great. I think that is possibly what pulls me up, and that's the main reason I want to stay in schools. I have been offered various jobs in the district, but I know that I just have to stay here. I love working with them. You could be down and they put their arms around you, and they are giving you support. And it's not easy to get this from middle school children, but I have such rapport with them. It fills you right up, so I know that's what keeps me going. That's really from the heart. I can walk in the hallways and see those faces, and it's the best."

With some distance from this experience, Nancy can say, "Well, one thing I know now is that I have to be much more conscious [about recognizing] my staff." She talked about how much she already was doing for the students. Now, however, she is making more of an effort to acknowledge the adults in school—by writing notes, by baking, by simply saying thank you. Being too busy is unacceptable; as she asserted: "I don't have time, but I make the time. My reward comes from people saying they like what I do. I think that is important. I enjoy what I do for myself, and so I am comfortable with that. But when I make or do things for teachers and they come back and say they really like that or thank you, that's what makes me feel good—that I have been able to show appreciation and they have felt my appreciation."

Equally important, Nancy said that telling her story helped her understand why she was so hurt. After puzzling over this strange emotional event in her career, she realized that she does indeed need recognition from others, especially her own supervisors. She added that she felt lucky that, for her, talking to someone about a problem is a way to let go of her anger and move on to something else.

Visiting her again one year after the initial interview and two years following the wounding incident, we found an exuberant leader bursting with *joie de vivre* and busily preparing to open a new school. Nancy had received the recognition she needed from the district. She had been personally invited to apply and was handily selected to be principal of a newly built middle school. The pain of nonrecognition had evaporated, replaced by an eye on the future and a softening of past hurts. In her words: "When they called me and wanted me to be principal and said 'We know you can do it, you are the one we want,' I felt very good. My district wanted me to open up a brand-new school, and I really felt good about that. I was flattered. So that's why I'm thinking I took one little isolated incident and let that hurt me. Now with the overall picture, I have been totally supported by the district."

Trying to make sense of what happened, she said, "I think, in our job, given the things we are involved with, it is inevitable that we are going to be hurt. Because we can't always be supported in our beliefs, especially when we are dealing with so many different personalities, the parents, the students. And we make decisions, we say things, and if it's not supported you do feel wounded, whether it's a large wound or a small wound. But I reflect on all the good things and know that it's not me personally. I just think the system is so big and there are so many things happening. I am as guilty as the district for not recognizing the teachers for the little things, saying thank you enough. I am doing it on a smaller scale, and I don't know why my expectations for the district were to do things differently. But I think that's the way I really look at it now. It may hurt, it may bother me for a little bit, but I am convinced that it will never get me down."

The challenge for this principal was to accept trials as part of the leadership adventure and use them to learn. She had to identify obstacles that prevented her from listening to her own needs. When we left Nancy, she was wiser about her needs, big and small, and was better at finding balance in her life. She summed up her learning this way: "It is a journey. I think the more we do, the more we learn, the more we grow. It leads to new adventures."

9

Dancing on the Skillet

The day Christopher was appointed superintendent of Valhalla schools, he was in his glory. This district was where he began his career as a teacher, and now he was returning years later to be its chief school officer. He recalled, "It was a moment like few others in a person's life. In a lot of ways, it was the realization of a dream." When he was installed in his new position, "It set the tone for what I had at that point in time thought was going to be, I suppose naïvely, forever and ever, amen. It was one of the high points of my life. Now I'm officially the leader at a place that I dearly love, with family and friends near by. It doesn't get much better than that.

"So life was good. We were cutting the deficit. Enrollment was up. I was happy. I had gotten married. We had a beautiful daughter. We were in the process of planning for another child. And life . . . I would have to say it was at the crest of the wave. The dream had come true. I remember pinching myself every once in a while: Can this be real? This is too good to be true. I was deliriously happy.

"I remember going to a conference and seeing a lot of people from my new superintendents' class, half a dozen of whom had already been fired or quit. At that point, the average life expectancy of a school superintendent was three and a half years; it was a period when life was short for school leaders. A couple of my colleagues had already been canned or were on their way out, but I thought *I'm so lucky because I love my school, I love my board, I love my kids. I* was feeling really good about everything I did. The board, the school, my personal life was cooking right along, I was deliriously happy with the baby. So, I was pumped. But! [laughter] Maybe that's a good place to pause!"

But a crisis was waiting in the wings. At the time Christopher began his fourth year as superintendent, "Things had started to erode internally. Ah, some new faces on the board. A new board chair came in—a person with whom I did not see eye to eye very often, a very different style from my first board chair. I'll never forget: Olivia and I were expecting Ian, and the new board chair and I were supposed to go to Washington for a meeting about leadership and partnership. And I had to cancel at the last minute because Olivia was going into labor. Ian was on the way. The board chair never, never, never forgave me. He never forgot about it. When I was resigning, he said, 'I knew it wasn't going to work when you canceled that meeting to go to Washington.' So we got off on the wrong foot. We had a tough time."

Christopher found that he was running the district according to the demands of other people, especially the new chairman of the board. Anxious to keep his beloved position, he said that he tried his best to satisfy the board but kept getting into conflict: "I was becoming increasingly weary of some of the politics, of feeling unsupported and second-guessed by my board chair." To complicate matters further, the board was shifting its vision for the district, and the new direction did not please Christopher. "I clearly wanted to move in one direction, and they clearly wanted to move in another, and OK, never the twain shall meet." Yet he continued to try to please the board and do what they asked.

The situation worsened. While tensions mounted between Christopher and the new board, he was suddenly faced with a major budget shortfall. He was blamed for this and all its negative repercussions and said, "Things appeared to be unraveling. I was trying to keep my finger in the dike. Confidence in me was eroding, even from my supporters. And they wanted to see if I could 'manage my way out of this.'" He worried about losing his power base in the community.

Coincidentally, the district was in the middle of a major public outreach campaign. Christopher told us, "My wife and I had almost no private life. We were always entertaining. All for the good of the district. Olivia and I talked a little bit, and I said, 'I'm miserable. I'm just not happy. I'm tired of fighting the fight.'

"I didn't feel that I was physically strong enough to survive another year. And I, I was just a mess, miserable. I don't want to say depressed, maybe I was, I don't know, but I didn't want to see people. A lot of people asked me, 'What's the matter with you? You're not yourself.' I was so preoccupied, consumed by school stuff. So I thought, well I've got to get my life back. I said, 'I'm going to gamble and take a year, and I'll try to get a job.'"

Christopher resigned. He negotiated a year off with pay to have time to consider the next step. Eventually he accepted a new position as principal of Hudson School, located in another state. That's where we met for the interviews.

Reflecting on the experience, he said: "And so I think sometimes I may have—in my eagerness to be the superintendent there— allowed them to direct me in a way that I really didn't believe in, but did because it was good for me or good for my career . . . and I thought I could maybe change it once I got going on it. And that turned out not to be the case."

After the board changed, he told us, "there were days when I was so angry and depressed—I guess that's not the right word. Busting my tail, but for what? I was underappreciated, undervalued. This made me not happy at home. There were days when I didn't think I would survive. That I'd end up in an early grave. Olivia said I walked like this [slumped, bent over]. So that's my sad tale."

Somewhere along the way, he became fearful of losing his job and was so intent on satisfying the board that he discovered his grip on leadership was slipping. When leaders go too far to please others, as Christopher said happened to him, they may start to distance themselves from who they want to be as leaders. Christopher lost sight of himself. Also, boundaries between career and family blurred so much that he neglected his family.

As he related it: "So that dream got broken and things looked grim, but the sun comes up tomorrow! It's what we tell our kids. I picked myself up, dusted myself off, and looked at alternatives. I'm better off now. People ask, 'Do you want to be superintendent again?' I feel fine, OK with what I do. Is it perfect, do I get everything I need? No, but I don't think that you ever do. It's OK. It works." Courted to be a superintendent again, Christopher told us he was flattered, but he said, "No. I want to stay right here for a while. I don't want to say 'lick my wounds' but, I think, sort of get back on track. Every once in a while, I get a little itchy for the superintendency again, being in the larger venue where I'm more a direct player in the decision-making process. Then I step back and say, 'Hmm, do I really want that?' Because all those things come at a price.

"I think that for me and for Olivia and for the kids, this is where I need to be right now. We have a life. I work hard, but I have time for my family, for my friends again. And I get to do some things that I haven't done in a long time. I get to teach again. I get to be with kids. I get to go to soccer games and cross-country meets. I mean, I just didn't have time for that. So when weighed, I think life is good. This is a good place to be. And at some point—when the children are a little bit older, maybe—think differently about my career again. It's a time-out period for me, maybe. Get my health back, my life on track. It's been a healthy period."

Christopher told us how the experience has changed his ideas about leadership. "I guess I've taken a whole different view of leadership. It's been a kind of transformation that says, If I'm doing my job well and effectively, and I'm true to myself and my career goals, to my philosophy of what education is for kids, the leadership falls into place quite naturally. Having gone through the experience and come out of it . . . I wouldn't say jaded, but the better for it . . . I see leadership a little differently now. And it needs to be more natural. I do what I have to do, and I do the right thing for the school, for kids, for me. And as a result, I'm more comfortable in the whole role of being 'a leader.' I don't have to try to be a leader, if that makes any sense. And I watch it here and at some other places, people who are trying to get that first principalship or that first division head job, they're scrambling around, almost playing at the role of being school leader. . . . To a degree, that's good. But relax a little bit. Be more yourself, and I think the long-term benefits will be better.

"For the first time in a long, long time, I think I'm pretty comfortable with who I am as an educator, with who I am as a leader. So I think that's probably the healthiest thing that's come out of this. I have reached a level of maturity, whatever you want to call it. I don't have to press. This is who I am and what I am. I guess my focus is less on my career and more on who I am as a person. The kind of husband and father I want to be. And the kind of educator I want to be. And that supersedes the career goal. For a while, I was more career-goal-oriented. I wanted to be a school superintendent. And that tended to be the focus."

Christopher said he learned from this experience: "It was an adventure. I feel very fortunate to have had that opportunity, as young as I had it. And most of that experience was very, very good. We focused on some of the pain. But we learned a lot of great life lessons there. And I'll always be grateful for that piece of my life. I guess it's part of being a lifelong learner. You benefit from every experience that you have. I think I benefited. Does that mean I'm complacent in my career? No, I don't mean to imply that. I'm not settling. I'm just at a good place, feeling good about it. Take the time to enjoy it and do it well.

"I feel to some degree I'm in control of my life where I hadn't been in control. Other people had too much to say about how and when you do things. And maybe that's not true of all school leaders. Maybe I let people have too much control. But regardless, I'm happy with my station in life right now. And I think because of that it translates to my leadership style.

"But I do think it's possible to be truer to myself as a school leader than I was the first time through. I was just so, 'I want it' [said in stage whisper] . . . knowing that I was answerable to that board. Knowing that they hire and fire the superintendent, the superintendent hires and fires everybody else. I was always dancing on the skillet.

"But, you know, some things got put in place during my watch. And I have to frame it in the context that says, 'Well, that's good. It fits in the overall scheme of the place.' Had I not been there, maybe it wouldn't have happened the way it did. So I keep looking for the positive things. And I've become less and less bitter. I've been able to let go of it."

Christopher tells a story of how he eventually accepted and sought to use the leadership crisis. The meaning of the uninvited interruption in his career path was not immediately apparent, but given time, distance, and reflection, he now believes that he has benefited. He tells how in the beginning he tried to fix the problem, but it would not go away and only got worse. As problems deepened, he couldn't deny them and was compelled to respond. This muddle was not part of his plan, yet it couldn't be ignored. He reported that he was becoming emotionally, socially, and physically drained. Bombarded by threats from the outside, he wondered if he was becoming depressed. Meaning was gradually revealed to him as he wrestled retrospectively with what happened and considered what this meant for him as an educator.

Interestingly, he does not want to return to who he was before the crisis. He has moved on and in a sense has reinvented himself. The critical events became a foundation for personal change and growth. By the end of the story, he is a man who is much less concerned with living according to others' expectations for leaders, and more focused on how he sees himself. He has reconciled who he is with how others see him and feels satisfaction in knowing that he is now truer to his own beliefs and values. He speaks of being transformed as a leader, and as a family man. In the story, we witness a changed individual, a man who has repossessed his past and redeemed himself. Although he could not say this while living the horror of his crisis, today he appreciates what happened. He recognizes that it gave something to him that has made him different, perhaps stronger, perhaps wiser, certainly changed.

Some people will interpret Christopher's narrative to be a story of failure, but he does not see it that way. He said he could be licking his wounds but is not. The losses stemming from the crisis were used as an opportunity to look at himself and his life from the inside out. In a sense, he lost and found himself; the self has returned. As he and his story have developed, he has found a voice and uses it to tell others about his leadership journey. He reported he will remember never to separate humanity from the organization, and to lead with dignity and grace, whatever job title he assumes. The position is now less important than the work. Maybe he will find that he wears his leadership better in this different role. Maybe not.

At the point we left Christopher's story, he acknowledged that he is changed and is confident about who he will become, even though he's not sure what it is other than that he will be faithful to his own values and beliefs. Like the individual who suffers a devastating medical illness but talks about how he feels more alive than ever, Christopher reflected: "I think I was pretty good at most of it. Did I have some faults? Yeah, I think I was much too eager to try to please people. It's big-time different. It really is. . . . It's that seasoning, you gotta go through it. Bottom line, am I better for having had the entire experience? Absolutely."

Part III

Looking for the Good Story

10

Narrative Healing
Once Upon a Time

Stories are all around us. Storytelling is what people do. Story is one of the most fundamental forms of communication; it is our "universal gift" (Coles, 1989, p. 30). We "dream in narrative, daydream in narrative, remember, anticipate, hope, despair, believe, doubt, plan, revise, criticize, construct, gossip, learn, hate and live by narrative," observed Barbara Hardy (1977, p. 13). Leaders are no exception; the narrative form of story is central to what they do and who they are.

The so-called craft knowledge that leadership "war stories" offer has been well documented (Barth, 1990; Witherell and Noddings, 1991) and proven to be valuable for a variety of reasons: for the teller's reordering and sense making in difficult situations, and as teaching and learning for others. Jackson (1995) asserted that stories, fiction and nonfiction, *"transform* us, alter us as individuals" (p. 9; italics in original). Using narrative to make sense of one's own and others' experience has been applied by psychologists (Bruner, 1986, 1987; Coles, 1989; Polkinghorne, 1988) and philosophers (Egan, 1989; MacIntyre, 1981; Ricoeur, 1984). Likewise, narratives have found useful applications in educational research (Elbaz, 1990; Clandinin and Connelly, 1990). Our fundamental interest, however, is in the *story within the story,* what Schaefer (1992) called "self-story" or the self-narrative (Huberman, 1995)—that is, the self that is being formed in what is being told.

Underlying our book is a premise that the story form is a dominant sense-making tool for school administrators (Ackerman, Donaldson, and van der Bogert, 1996). Through telling, practitioners recreate their experience. They reflect and interpret. By telling a story, leaders can endow their experience with meaning. The "storied nature of human conduct" (Sarbin, 1986) is an idea that burgeoned rapidly in the literature; we find that there is growing interest in how people deal with experience by constructing stories.

Leader stories are a form of "situated knowledge" (Lave and Wenger, 1991) and, as such, represent a vital yet often misunderstood dimension of learning and sharing of practice. In this perspective, administrative knowledge does not necessarily denote exemplary thought and practice. It does, however, conceive of learning as an aspect of culturally and historically situated activity (Lave, 1996) and thus refers to social, cognitive, and emotional structures and administrative activities that are sometimes shared, sometimes idiosyncratic, and sometimes open to question. This kind of story knowledge represents a unification of personal knowledge and experience.

We have focused, then, on school leaders' *narrative identity* (Ricoeur, 1984), attempting to determine who in each case the person had become in the story, how the story helped him or her become that person, and why. By bearing witness to the leaders' stories, we acknowledge and name leadership wounding. By naming what the leader was feeling as a wound, a new relationship between leader and the trial of leadership is formed.

Stories of Restitution, Chaos, and Quest

The wound can be an opening to a leader's own true story, and the story can be told in a variety of forms. How a leader chooses to frame her story offers insight into how she interprets her experience. In studying people who are wounded, Frank (1995) used three narrative structures to translate human suffering into stories: restitution, chaos, and quest. We find this framework helpful when listening to a leader's first-person account of crisis. Each narrative type has a unique meaning. A person telling a restitution story expects that the crisis will be solved and life will return to the way it used to be, whereas an individual who tells a chaos story is trapped in the crisis and does not see a way out. The teller of a quest story uses the crisis as a way to change and grow, even if the problem is not fixed. Like most others, leaders tell a story of crisis that conforms to a recognizable plot line, such as restitution, chaos, and quest—a story that becomes their narrative truth.

Frank (1995) passionately argued that illness stories are self-stories and that the three narrative types offer insight into what the stories tell. Rather than fragmenting stories to support findings, he used the stories "to model theorizing—and living—with stories" (p. 23). He encouraged people to reshape his theory with their lived stories; we have tried to do that from the perspective of metaphorically wounded leaders. Furthermore, the seemingly distant literature of medical sociology offers insights into the inner landscape of the leader's life and has inspired us to examine the response of the wounded leader as wounded storyteller.

Frank described this typology in the context of narrative that is easily accessible to people: "A narrative type is the most general story-line that can be recognized underlying the plot and tensions of particular stories. People tell their own unique stories, but they compose these stories by adapting and combining narrative types that cultures make available" (p. 75). Frank warned, and we agree, that the framework is not the truth of the stories but instead offers a lens to focus on stories that have their own truth.

The idea of restitution, chaos, and quest constitutes a scaffolding for listening and for interpreting stories of leadership wounding. Moreover, viewing stories in the light of this kind of typology (there are others to explore) furnishes a way of looking at how the leader responds to a stressful wounding situation and how he develops his capacity for leadership.

When listening to a leader's story, we notice that one plot line predominates; however, it is likely that there are traces of all three types. Moreover, during the course of the wounding experience, the story weaves in and out of the themes of quest, restitution, and chaos. We begin our discussion with the restitution story.

Restitution

The line "yesterday I was healthy, today I'm sick, but tomorrow I'll be healthy again" (Frank, 1995, p. 77) captures the essence of the restitution story. The restitution narrative, as reflected in many leader stories, acknowledges the cataclysmic interruption that a crisis causes; at the same time, it anticipates and even expects an eventual end to the crisis. The school leader is able to resolve the potentially debilitating problem and return to life as it used to be. The restitution prognosis is optimistic.

Consider Joan, a fourth-year principal of an elementary school located in a suburban community, who opened her daily newspaper one morning to find the headline "JOAN WILLOW A DICTATOR!" The article, based on a letter that an irate parent in her school had sent to the newspaper, described a series of decisions that Joan had made regarding the parent's children, and the school program. A number of articles were subsequently published, prompted by the same parent, detailing further alleged misdeeds by Joan with yet another headline: "WILLOW WEAK AND DEFENSELESS." Joan described her reaction: "I value my reputation, certainly, but especially as a leader! People need to have confidence in your ability. There are parents who don't necessarily know me who are going to read this and think, hmmm . . . there is something else going on here. I didn't know this woman was like this."

Joan said she called her lawyer and superintendent to determine what she could do about the letters. She was told that as a semi-public official, she was "fair game." It would be difficult to argue or prove slander. Joan's reaction was as follows: "I had to back down, and it felt weird that I just had to wait and hope for other people to support me. I felt powerless. I felt slammed. It was unbelievable, it was very upsetting, I had a hard time sleeping. Oh, great, I'm a tyrant and weak and defenseless. In the meantime, I did feel powerless. I did feel defenseless, I *was*. I had to rely on other people to say, 'No, she's not that bad, she's not a tyrant.' And to choose that word when I take such pains to not be autocratic, to be collaborative, to work with people. . . . It was the antithesis of what I was. It didn't make me question what I was, I knew, but to have that in black and white in public, it was appalling—it was more than appalling. It was deeply upsetting, because really that article was not just about my leadership style, it was about who I am. It was saying publicly that I was someone that I'm definitely not, and I didn't want myself defined in that way. When you lose control of the definition, you have to depend on other people; someone has taken something very precious away."

Joan told us that a groundswell of support soon emerged from parents, teachers, students, and community groups to counter the charges leveled against her. Thereupon, the accusing parent wrote a letter of apology, followed by a meeting with Joan where the apology was rendered in person. Joan summed up, "There was a kind of redemption, and it was over."

The restitution narrative, as reflected in Joan's story, recognizes the disruption that these events caused; at the same time, it anticipates and even expects an eventual end to the crisis. Concomitantly, she saw the restitution of self, a bit scarred but determined to get on with her work. This restitution story and numerous others we heard show how leaders cope with difficult challenges and with their wounds. The leaders' wounds, as described to us, have been covered and protected, but they remain isolated from who they are as leaders, at least at that point in time.

What's missing from this kind of story as told is how the leader was changed by the experience. It may be comparable to when an individual gets hurt, say with a fractured arm, and it heals neatly, so the person can simply move on with life and the experience does not cause any change. The restitution presumption is that the wound will be cured. This is a culturally preferred narrative.

Storytellers and listeners like the restitution story. It expresses how a challenge was faced and is consistent with our cultural bias toward thinking of leaders as fixers. Even though the leader may not actually be the one who fixed the problem (as in Joan's story), the problem gets fixed and life goes on as usual for the leader.

This culturally preferred story, however, is not the only one. It assumes all problems can be fixed. It also keeps the focus on the outcome, which can deter the leader from returning to the source of the problem. This path away from the unknown shuts down an opportunity for learning, apart from knowing where to find the quick fix next time. What happens when a leader only knows the restitution story but, when wounded, does not attain restitution? It's easy to get stuck in a preferred story line.

Chaos

Sometimes, when a leader experiences a devastating wound, she becomes trapped in what Frank (1995) called a "chaos narrative." The restitution narrative expects an eventual return to life as it was; the chaos narrative envisions failure. Caught in the moment, the leader has lost her voice and is unable to reflect on what is happening. This kind of story is chaotic in its absence of narrative order. It is told as an event, without sequence or discernible causality. As Frank said when writing about people who are ill, "the story traces the edges of a wound that can only be told around" (p. 98).

These stories are not easy to hear. There is disassociation in the telling, as well as scattering of events, rationale, and circumstance that make it, we suspect, hard to hear as well as to tell. Also, similar to a physician who prefers to work with patients whose illness can be cured, there are educators who shun colleagues (and schools) where there is chaos and the promise of success is dim. A leader living in chaos is at risk of becoming abandoned. We found that these stories are also not easy to solicit, since the leaders are, understandably, often reluctant to talk (particularly to interviewers).

Harry's story approached a chaos narrative. Hearing his story was difficult. The chaos narrative depends on the view that no one is in control; to some extent, this seemed to be the case with Harry. He felt overwhelmed. According to Frank, someone actually living the chaos cannot form a story because he would have to have "a reflective grasp of it" (1995, p. 98). Having lived with the crisis for some time, Harry had just barely begun to find space for reflection.

He was a second-year principal of a middle school with a student body of five hundred students. He told us "a command style of leadership" seemed to be expected of him, but this was not his style. After a year and a half on the job, he found himself staring at his picture on the cover of the local newspaper; he was at the center of a litany of allegations and accusations that morale was at an all-time low, and that he was a principal who was "out of touch." He said he was not sure what to do and did not know what his future would be. He felt out of control: "When I came here, I believe they expected— and I'm beginning to understand it's probably in a lot of other places too—the command style of leadership—you do this, you do this, you do that. And *I am just not that way!!* I am just not that way. Then I tried to shape things a little differently, and it started by shaping how we handled faculty meetings and, uh, I had been coached a bit not to go too fast. Then I tried to have this notion of people speaking up, being able to formulate their own decisions, playing your own tune but being in a jazz band kind of thing. And I see some of that working now, but in the first eighteen months I asked people, when I first came, to host a faculty meeting in their own room. Before that, as I understand, they had gone down to the library and the principal set up the agenda and they checked it off. In that first eighteen months, that kind of eliciting from people was just so foreign. Where are these people? I don't know what I'm going to do."

When speaking with Harry, we found it unclear how events had gotten to that point and steps to control the sweep of events seemed to be contingent on things outside his domain.

Illness is often about learning to live with a loss of control, suggesting that the body (in the case of a medical wound) experiences a continuum starting from predictability and going to contingency at the opposite end. Contingency is the condition of being subjected to forces one thinks one cannot control. From the perspective of leadership, the narratives of Harry and Joan caused us to examine closely how leaders respond to lost predictability. Their respective stories, however, diverge along the narrative paths.

Like Harry, leaders who tell a chaos story talk about disaster or near disaster. The story is notable by what is absent: it is a distressed telling without order or coherence; the future is uncertain. The consequences of chaos to the individual leader and to the organization can be devastating.

Yet within chaos can come good. A leader, for example, may eventually find his way out of crisis and use the experience as the basis for change. When talking to leaders about fear of chaos, Parker Palmer offered another perspective: "The insight we receive on the inner journey is that chaos is the precondition to creativity: as every creation myth has it, life itself emerged from the void. Even what has been created needs to be returned to chaos from time to time so that it can be regenerated in more vital form" (2000, pp. 89–90). Harry did find success and self-fulfillment after he quit that position and secured a better-fitting role doing something entirely different in another work setting.

Chaos, then, brings opportunity and danger, for better or worse. We want to remember, however, that stories can change. Chaos stories may change to restitution, restitution stories may change to chaos, and in time they may become stories of quest.

Quest

A leader's story of quest is similar to the ill person who tells a story that is not necessarily about medicine's triumphs over disease, but rather of an individual who takes charge of his or her own story regardless of the medical outcome. They both believe that they are better for the experience despite obvious negative results, be it loss of a bodily organ or loss of a high-ranking job. Frank (1995) found that "quest stories meet suffering head on; they accept illness and seek to *use* it. Illness is the occasion of a journey that becomes a quest. What is quested for may never be wholly clear, but the quest is defined by the person's belief that something is to be gained through the experience" (p. 115; italics in original). This is a story of someone who, by accepting and confronting the pain, eventually finds meaning in suffering.

Consider again Christopher's story (featured in Chapter Nine). It is not as acute or dramatic, of course, as a life-threatening illness, but four years into what he considered the ultimate career as superintendent he found that he was running the district according to the demands of other people, especially the new chairman of the board. Anxious to keep his dream position, he said he tried his best to please the board, but this meant acting against his beliefs; he found he was disconnecting from people, including himself. There was too much distance between his values and how he lived. He eventually quit the job he dearly loved and the life he had devoted years trying to create. He found a way to roll up his sleeves and start over—began settling in to a new role, this time as principal—only to be dealt the blow of a heart attack; yet he was eventually able to say, "Bottom line, am I better for having had the entire experience? Absolutely."

He learned from the crisis and thinks differently about what it means to be a leader today. He brings this learning to his new position and has no expectation of returning to the status quo of life before the leadership crisis. In Parker Palmer's terms, Christopher has begun to listen to his own life: "Before you tell your life what you intend to do with it, listen for what it intends to do with you. Before you tell your life what truths and values you have decided to live up to, let your life tell you what truths you embody, what values you represent" (2000, p. 3). With better insight into himself, his particular set of strengths, talents, and beliefs, Christopher can say that he is now truer to himself and a more genuine leader.

The wound can be a call to consciousness, the wake-up call to learning and leadership growth. In counterpoint to Harry and Joan,

Christopher's story and the others found in Part Two demonstrate how leaders who tell a story of quest heed the call and face their pain. "Hiding from suffering only makes us more afraid," Rachel Remen (2000) wrote. "We avoid suffering only at the great cost of distancing ourselves from life. In order to live fully, we may need to look deeply and respectfully at our own suffering and at the suffering of others. In the depths of every wound we have survived is the strength we need to live. The wisdom our wounds can offer us is a place of refuge. Finding this is not for the faint of heart. But then, neither is life" (p. 138). Nor is leadership.

People telling a story of quest accept leadership crisis and find a way to use it; they change. They go beyond fixing the problem. In fact, some leaders, as we saw in Part Two, manage to fix the problem while others do not. However, all tell of varying degrees of personal and professional growth. They capitalize on a wounding experience and use it to seek new insights into themselves and their leadership.

These are leaders who become transformed as they quest for better ways of being a person, of being a leader. Leaders telling a story of quest do not want to, or perhaps cannot, return to who they were before the crisis; they are on a path to change. You could even say that some have reinvented themselves; they change their self-myth. For some, the change is simply about accepting who they have been all along; they become authentic. These are ordinary people who, in time, may become extraordinary. How? Like Joseph Campbell's hero with a thousand faces (1949), they summon the courage to take the first step and enter the unknown.

A Simple Form of Healing

The typology—restitution, chaos, and quest—ultimately is a helpful tool for hearing the story the leader is telling himself. This is a narrative framework that has been helpful in our work; there are likely many others. A story, of course, does not always fit neatly into one narrative type. People's lives and their stories are forever changing. The typology simply offers three bins that can aid interpretation of what the story means to the teller.

A story by itself is not a remedy for all that ails; nevertheless, story may represent the simplest and most elegant form of healing. Admittedly, this may be somewhat overstated. But we can say that after listening to many leaders tell their story of wounding to us and after observing numerous small groups of leaders telling and listening to each other's story, we recognize that something rather special can transpire when a good story is told. The simple, everyday act of telling a story can be a profound experience. When leaders share a story of crisis, they potentially gain insight into their leadership practice, enhanced self-awareness, empathy for other, and affirmation of self. If the storytelling and listening conditions are right, the experience can be powerful; there is promise of learning, growth, and healing. These ideas are developed further in the next chapter.

11

What Wounding Teaches

What is to be learned from the experience of wounding? It is on the path through the heart's most fragile territory where the lessons can be learned. Here they are:

- Learn to trust the unattended areas of your leadership—especially your feelings.

- Listen honestly and deeply for the questions that are feared or left out of your work life altogether.

- Find folks to talk to whom you really trust.

These lessons suggest a direction for leadership development; we approach them here from several angles. First, our discussion considers some of the conditions necessary to make room for the emotional development and intelligence of the person and the personal, amid all the roles, pressures, and wounds we have described in the context of leadership. Second, we consider the challenges and opportunities for the school leader to sustain a healthy questioning and conversational spirit. Finally, we offer an outline (certainly not exhaustive) of some commonsense ideas about how to link practitioners to each other and how to engage leaders both cognitively and affectively, all with the goal of leaders finding their own unique path to personal and professional fulfillment.

Don't Do Something; Just Be There

In 1974, Donn Kesselheim wrote a paper titled "A Rationale for Out-door Activity as Experiential Education: The Reason for Freezin'"; it was intended to probe the learning processes involved in the work of outdoor education programs such as Outward Bound. Kesselheim argued that the primary outcome of outdoor education was to "en-hance self-concept, that is, to bring about greater understanding of the self, so that students would acquire insight into their strengths and weaknesses" (cited in James, 1980, p. 116). Walsh and Golins (1976) extended the idea by developing a model that they elegantly reduced to a single proposition: a learner is placed in a unique phys-ical environment and then given a characteristic set of problem-solving tasks and impelled into a state of disequilibrium or dissonance to which she may or may not adapt, potentially reorganizing the meaning and direction of her experience.

Most veterans of outdoor experiential education programs (we count ourselves among them) can tell the tale of at least one adven-ture that reflected this essential idea. A memorable one occurred for one of us while rock climbing on what at first glance seemed to be a friendly, modest-looking mountain. That initial perception changed dramatically some two hundred feet above the ground, where the notion of finding another handhold in otherwise smooth granite seemed like an impossibility at the time. Given the height, the tired-ness, the terror, and the general way the mind screams out "Get me down. I don't want to be here. I can't do it!" it is important to note as the story unfolds that being stranded on a small mountain can have no parallel to the suffering of a life-threatening illness. Pro-grams such as Outward Bound rely on a clever and important notion called "perceived risk" to make things seem riskier than they really are. The safety ropes and features that hold one to a mountain, as well as the superb training of the instructors, are extraordinarily comprehensive and carefully calibrated to keep one "safe." Never-theless, most alumni of such programs will testify that such preventives offer little solace at the time; perception of risk and imminent harm (and death) seems real when you are there.

First, there is, of course, everything that got you up the mountain—every part of your will, desire, fear, imagination, and stupidity that put you on a granite ledge high enough in the air to kill you if you fall. Then, there is the noble core philosophy of groups like Outward Bound, which state you can do something you have never done before and you can do it by "adapting"—that is, by changing your mind-set, trying, and maybe succeeding. There is your instructor and everyone else watching patiently and expectantly from below, as you cling to impossibly shallow granite handholds and footholds. Frantic with desperation, you try to will the rock to do your bidding, holding it so tightly you think you can move it and make it do what you want. Your whole world is reduced to the four narrow crevices in which you've reluctantly trusted your hands and feet. It doesn't seem at all reasonable to stay on the rock in this fashion for very long. Your line of vision is reduced to about six inches in front of you, to the side, down (if you dare), and up. Then you hear from below: "Hey, Ackerman, you can't beat up that rock. You've got to be gentle. You gotta learn to dance with it." Those words don't make a lot of sense at the time (but many years later, they do). What the instructor means is that you must find a way to lean out away from the rock—a totally counterintuitive move—despite everything telling you to lean into the rock, grab it, hold it, cling to it for dear life. You either want to go up (find the friggin' handhold that will save your life, hoist you up, and get it over with) or down (slowly and carefully lower yourself by the rope all the way down to the safety of the firm ground where you started, and be prepared to suffer the understanding and sympathetic looks of your colleagues and instructor regarding what you know is your failure). These seem like the only choices.

The advice from the ground (from Parsifal), from your instructor, is telling you to go the other way: stay in the "in between" (Chödrön, 2001) place, by which he means, again, "dance and laugh with the rock." He says: become more intimate with the queasy feeling of being in the middle of nowhere. These do not seem like real options at all, but they really are. Here is the thing: you just cannot look graceful on that rock. You actually must look a little bit foolish, awkward, and vulnerable; if you are lucky, you have an opportunity to see something of your wound. The wound is not the mountain; it is simply how you decide to respond to the situation. The real learning, most Outward Bound instructors would say, comes in being able to relax in that moment and just be there.

We fully recognize that the terror involved in this modest adventure story pales next to some of the stories you have heard in the previous chapters, but the metaphor is designed to make a point. It might be what the Fisher King understands when Parsifal asks the question, or what so many illness narratives say between the lines, and what we have heard in our stories: in fact, there is really nothing to hold on to. There is simply the state of being right in between the action we think we need to take to run from the situation, and the comfort of staying in the place that is familiar. This place in the middle is usually a place we want to avoid because it looks like inaction, indecision—the bane of a leader's existence. It is, however, an example of "holding the paradox" (Chödrön, 2001; Johnson, 1991) or what Parker Palmer (1998) called the tension of opposites. It is just being there and being able to see what is happening.

So much of the language of leadership is doing and action. The potential stance on the mountain suggests otherwise: "Don't do something; just be there." It has been described nicely by Robert Johnson as a highly conscious waiting (1991). To find the next handhold prematurely is perhaps to miss an opportunity. To simply be able to stay in that moment for even an instant is what Buddhists call "meeting the enemy" (Chödrön, 2001), which is seeing ourselves without deception, the essence of what some call bravery. The enemy, in this sense, is supposed to be the good teacher, showing us those parts of ourselves we fail to see or fail to know. So, staying in this in-between state on the mountain requires, among other things, a certain tolerance for uncertainty, ambiguity, and insecurity (an important trait for leaders as well). In the terminology of Outward Bound, it is getting beyond your comfort zone, although the zone here is not only physical; it is mental and emotional.

Indoor Education: The Emotional Life of the Leader

A school is, essentially, an indoor education program; it has the potential to provide an emotional Outward Bound for the school leader. Many leaders feel the equivalent of these same physical challenges in their own wounds. Many must struggle productively with the disequilibrium around them. There are, as we have already described in another context, modestly large boulders and mountains on the ground floor of schools—dissonant conditions—that make adaptation a challenging prospect for the leader.

Conflict and dilemma are a constant and natural part of leadership life, as are leadership wounds, and they may even be useful. Michael Fullan and Matthew Miles (1992) said "problems are our friends," encouraging the leader to embrace them in that "avoidance of real problems is the enemy of productive change because it is these problems that must be confronted for breakthroughs to occur" (p. 750). Fullan (1998) went further, exhorting the practitioner to "move toward the danger." Karolyn Snyder, Michele Acker-Hocevar, and Kristen Snyder (2000) echoed this view and proposed a theory of organizational change they called living on the edge of chaos; it included disequilibrium as a key element. They claimed that "disequilibrium rather than stability stimulates the system to respond in the most dynamic, fundamental, and noticeable ways. The leadership task is to use information to stimulate disequilibrium, which provides energy for change" (p. 84).

Educational orthodoxy tends to overlook many of these issues—in particular, the role of emotion in the work of leadership (and in the classroom). Nevertheless, the concept of emotion is fast becoming central to many issues of contemporary leadership. Emotion literally means "disturbance" (Hillman, 1997) and comes from the Latin *emovere*, meaning "to disturb." Emotional disturbance, as such, seems to be a natural and inevitable part of leadership life and obviously becomes quite pronounced in crisis. Howard Gardner (1993), who developed the idea of personal intelligence that incorporates human emotion, claimed that "the less a person understands his own feelings, the more he will fall prey to them" (p. 254). Gardner added that on the other side of the coin, "the less a person understands the feelings, the responses, and the behavior of others, the more likely he will interact inappropriately with them and therefore fail to secure his proper place within the larger community" (p. 254).

So many of the school leaders interviewed and followed for this book were self-described "emotionally scarred" veterans who experienced crisis of various kinds in their leadership role. It is clear that the most essential quality leaders must have is to know who they are and what they stand for—what Daniel Goleman (1995) described as "self-awareness," or the ability to recognize and understand one's moods, emotions, and drives, as well as their effect on others. The stories in Part Two posed a number of examples and questions to consider with respect to the emotional life of school leaders. How do leaders attune themselves to building relationships? How do they emotionally understand the interpersonal dynamics that constitute those relationships? To what extent are leaders able to understand behavioral, verbal, and expressive cues and deduce the emotional states of those around them (Donaldson, 2001)?

Underlying the capacity to foster relationships are two critical qualities: success at forming authentic relationships, and in turn intrapersonal self-awareness (Donaldson, 2001). Such a skill set requires gauging accurately how our behaviors are received and perceived by others and, concomitantly, discussing and mediating with others feelings of fear, uncertainty, and even hostility that our behaviors might provoke. This is usually where the emotional truth (Goleman, 1995) is to be found, or what Goleman calls "marshaling emotions in the service of the goal" (p. 43).

Enhanced intrapersonal and interpersonal awareness constitutes an important direction toward sustaining emotional commitment to leadership work. For example, Sharon's story, in Chapter Six, reflects the journey of a person becoming more confident in her own interpersonal skills, a confidence dependent on having a growing intrapersonal awareness, to trust her own intuition and feelings about people, as well as awareness of their ideas and beliefs. In Sharon's story, her eventual ability to cultivate relationships stemmed far more from nonverbal, interpersonal qualities that she discovered than from cognitive, verbal, or philosophical positions. One of the benefits of paying attention to emotion is identification of one's own complex feelings in situations like Sharon's, and the self-reward for this behavior that can be found in the newly acquired affirmation from others.

Another challenge of emotional work is the ability to be responsive in practice to the culture of schools. In this sense, emotional intelligence requires understanding unstructured information gained through interaction with others, and avoiding what Argyris and Schön called "self-sealing theories-of-action" (1974, p. 161). A leader's operating theory of leadership (theory-of-action) may result in "self-sealing processes" (unquestioned action, behavior, and so forth) when assumptions are not tested and the leader is not open to change. Leaders choose how much to respond to the culture; many want to learn only as much about the culture as they need in order to impose their own conception of what they think is happening.

Readers may recall Carlos, from Chapter Seven, who imposed his own self-sealing theory-of-action. He closed himself from even considering other ways to respond to teachers and the tense situation. His theory-of-action had to be disconfirmed by sharing directly observable data and information with others, along with testing attributions made about others. For some leaders like Carlos, the need to feel essential or be in control can make listening for emotional cues difficult. As Donaldson (2001) suggested, this kind of need can overpower interpersonal sensitivity and propel the leader toward unilateral action. Emotional awareness of self and others can help leaders be open to a course of action that may not be what they would have chosen but may be best for the organization.

For ages, we have heard that one must be objective when making decisions—meaning, keep emotion separate from analysis. This is believed by some to be especially critical during times of crisis. Management courses typically encourage students to be rational; they suggest techniques ranging from simple plus-and-minus columns to complex decision-making trees, to reduce the possibility of emotion interfering with a decision. Yet the research of Antonio Damasio (1994) showed how, for better or worse, emotions are critical to the processes of reasoning and decision making.

An expert on emotion and feeling, neurologist Damasio reported cases of patients who suffered damage to specific areas of the brain. Although these individuals were completely rational prior to injury, afterward "they lost a certain class of emotions and, in a momentous parallel development, lost their ability to make rational decisions" (1999, p. 41), despite no change in cognitive ability. Damasio suggested that "emotion probably assists reasoning, especially when it comes to personal and social matters involving risk and conflict" (pp. 41–42), yet also insisted that emotions are not a substitute for reason, nor do emotions decide for us. "It is obvious that emotional upheavals can lead to irrational decisions. The neurological evidence simply suggests that selective absence of emotion is a problem. Well-targeted and well-deployed emotion seems to be a support system without which the edifice of reason cannot operate properly. These results and their interpretation called into question the idea of dismissing emotion as a luxury or a nuisance or a mere evolutionary vestige. They also make it possible to view emotion as an embodiment of the logic of survival" (p. 42). Damasio's brain research challenged the common belief that leaders should think dispassionately. He was not, however, saying that we should abandon reason and go with the gut ("somatic markers"). Instead, he shed light on how our emotional memory works: on the basis of prior experience and how we classify it, emotion can bias a decision one way or another, for good or bad.

School leaders, like all educators, require the means for sustaining and enhancing their emotional life in the face of daunting tasks and challenges. An administrator derives much of his or her motivation and satisfaction through intrinsic means, as we saw with leaders portrayed in the middle chapters; the administrator needs to be mindful of emotional and latent (unintended) skills in the service of leadership. Sensitivity to and understanding of the emotional nuances of leading is critical to the sense that leadership work is worth doing not simply for what is to be accomplished but for the sustaining aspects of the work itself.

Leadership development is slowly coming to acknowledge the importance of the emotional side of leadership. A person inhabits leadership. Ideally, one learns to live fully in and with each of one's feelings and reactions, making use of all one's organic equipment to sense, as accurately as possible, the situation within and without. This is, perhaps, the fully functioning leader, able to experience his feelings, engaged in the process of being and becoming himself.

Why Can't We Just Talk About This?

A principal of a large urban high school told this story. The school had been closed for two days on account of a severe snowstorm blanketing the city. When the school finally opened, the principal, as was his custom, arrived at 6:00 A.M. to start his day. Around 7:00, teachers started arriving. At one point, the principal came out of his office to the copier machine, where there stood a teacher who seemed quite perplexed and agitated. He asked if he could help. The teacher looked at him and immediately started yelling quite loudly, "What's the matter with this damn machine? It never works properly. It's out of toner. I'm so sick of this shit!" The principal stared at the teacher for a long moment. Then he said in a quiet and somewhat plaintive tone, "It is seven o'clock in the morning. Why are you yelling at me? Can't we just talk about this?"

This conversation, at one level, is so innocuous, yet unfortunately so typical in our experience. It speaks loudly about how conversations take place in the school. Why is it that principals and teachers often find themselves acting out of prescribed roles in their interaction? What prevents people from simply stepping out from behind themselves, as this principal did to "meet" one person openly and honestly? Many school leaders are quite familiar with the meeting after the faculty meeting, the one that takes place in the parking lot, where the real things somehow get talked about and the real work gets done. Educators who attend professional conferences often find that the best conversations and the highest learning take place on the way to the meeting rooms, in the bar, and over lunch. Why?

Schools tend to be organized with a stunning focus on function. Projects, methods, models, meetings, and memos tend to infect the language and culture of the school. This functional language exercises a powerful influence on people's relationships to each other. People in schools have become so familiar with this kind of talking (with each other) that it is an arrangement that permits the routine to continue without offering any challenges or nourishment. It is a pervasive and subtle form of human alienation in organizational life. Isaacs said, "One of the fundamental struggles for any leader stems directly from the separation that most of us feel between who we are as people and what we do as practical professionals" (1999, p. 3).

Evidence suggests that it can be different. Good conversation has powerful implications for the organizational culture of the school. How we think affects how we talk, and how we talk affects how we act and relate. Kegan and Lahey's book *How the Way We Talk Can Change the Way We Work* (2001) develops the idea that work settings are "language communities" (p. 7) consisting of mental transformative languages that have the capacity to radically influence organizational forms and functions. A corollary premise, the authors argued, is that leaders lead language communities and as such "have a choice whether to be thoughtful and intentional about this aspect of our leadership, or whether to unmindfully ratify the existing drift of our community's favored forms" (p. 8). We saw this at work in the stories profiled in our middle chapters.

Case Story

In our own work with educational leaders, we have used a simple approach we call *case story* as an intervention specifically to structure a safe environment for telling stories about critical events and generally to encourage a different kind of conversation among practitioners (see Appendix B). This approach coalesces a number of strategies that potentially help structure conditions for good talk and listening to occur (Jentz and Wofford, 1979).

The case story, a blend of case teaching and storytelling, serves as a personal and communal construct. It calls for a kind of critical thinking and feeling in an open and safe environment, one in which participants are, in effect, working out issues that they may not understand or may not have thought about or ever talked about. As a personal construct, it begins with the story we are telling ourselves. Next it opens people up to one another, for better or worse. With discipline, a connection can be made for the better; people can start to "listen for" the story that someone is telling them, rather than simply "listening to" the story.

It takes a certain kind of courage to have a conversation about oneself and one's leadership wounds. Talking and telling are not so simple to do; neither is listening. Becoming a storyteller is a way to recover a voice that painful, career-threatening dilemmas took away. In a conversation, "the teller not only has the potential to recover her voice; she becomes a witness to the conditions that rob others of their voices" (Frank, 1995, p. xii–xiii). When a person finds her voice, others can hear themselves in the story. None of these processes can be coerced or legislated; they have their own life and find their own way within a conversation and a person. Thus listening and listening well has astonishing benefits; by "join[ing] a living conversation . . . we may find ourselves wiser, more receptive, more understanding, nurtured, and sometimes even healed" (Witherell, Tran, and Othus, 1995, p. 41).

Many today are thinking about crafting anew conditions for conversation. For example, there is the noteworthy work done with critical friends groups and tuning protocols accomplished through the Coalition of Essential Schools and the Annenberg Institute for School Reform (Alan, Blythe, and Powell, 2001; McDonald, 1996). These conversational formats and others permit (and some even require) a new voice, a stepping beyond the conventional language and expression that usually hold ideas, thoughts, and feelings in place, leading potentially to significantly different and transformative levels of engagement and connection for participants.

The Sacred Question: Why Are You Wounded?

In our focus groups, classes, and workshops with wounded leaders, we have also been influenced by Parker Palmer's work (1998) and that of David Hagstrom (1998–99) with the "clearness committee" as a means of crafting a powerful conversation aimed at collective personal and professional growth. Palmer has adopted a traditional Quaker practice to use with teachers and administrators, the clearness committee, structured so that people can help each other by using a rather disciplined approach to conversation. A central principle of clearness work is learning to ask honest, open questions. Palmer said, "The best single mark of an honest, open question is that the questioner could not possibly anticipate the answer to it" (p. 153). A goal of the clearness committee, then, is not to solve the person's problem but rather to help the person whose issue is the focus of discussion "discover wisdom within . . . allowing the person to hear more clearly the guidance that comes from within" (pp. 153–154).

It is truly remarkable to witness the powerful transformations that can take place in clearness work, as much for questioners as for the focus person. The process requires a number of critical elements that involve willingness to communicate clearly and honestly; change one's mind-set; submit dearly held beliefs, feelings, and preconceptions to the questions of a group; use silence constructively; and trust the process. At the heart of the entire conversation is the genuine spirit of Parsifal at work. Much of the success of clearness work depends on artful asking of the question—the sacred question, what Joseph Campbell described as the "call to awakening." A reminder of a detail from the Fisher King story is important here. Parsifal need only ask the question; he is not required to answer it (Johnson, 1993, p. 47). It is the simple act of asking the question that marks the "consent to consciousness."

There is stunning power in asking the right question; as is the case with Parsifal's innocent fool, in a clearness conversation it is often lodged in an unexpected place. Sometimes the very question that can help another person unlock the wound is not one that is expected. There is remarkable healing power in listening to your voice tell your story and hearing it through others. Most participants in clearness work eventually come to see their own story as part of a larger story, understanding that their work and their wound belong to that larger story. This is also what heals. We continue to marvel at the imaginative and capricious qualities of Parsifal at work in this work. At the conclusion of a Leadership and Learning Clearness seminar with graduate students at Lewis and Clark College, David Hagstrom said, "This experience taught us to abandon the pretense that we know what is best for others. We learned that we must help others find their own answers. What we do need are good, honest, and direct questions that cause us to think about our situations differently" (p. 57).

In structured conversation like the case story or the clearness committee, the conversation is the relationship itself; the challenge is always to make that conversation more real. Defensiveness and division have the potential to collapse and give way to genuine participation and sharing. We have seen this happen in our workshops with astounding regularity. This sharing of mind, of consciousness, is oftentimes even more important than the content of the conversation. It may be that the content is limited anyway and the answer is not in the content at all, but somewhere else! There may be no answer! That is why conversational storytelling and listening in this way can be such a remarkable transforming experience. By offering individual perspectives in an environment where judgments are not expressed, it is possible to glimpse a broad vision of reality and to experience a participatory way of thinking. By learning to ask questions that lead to new levels of understanding, each person pushes the learning of the group. One becomes potentially more conscious of one's own and others' rational processes and of the points that separate or unite a group. Ultimately, by learning to develop a more embodied voice and converse in a way that decelerates the rhythm of habitual talk, the conversation can lead to a real, shared perception; greater sensitivity; and a larger, more generative language for understanding oneself and others.

The Screw-Up Hall of Fame

This kind of conversation might happen more often if there were less shame and taboo surrounding leadership wounds, similar to what we see happening today with issues of death and dying and the growth of the hospice movement. U.S. society has tended to avoid talking about ordinary people facing death. Today, matters of disease and mortality are debated regularly in journalism, courts, and legislatures, and there is an expanding literature of medical memoirs. Consider again the immense popularity of the book and television movie *Tuesdays with Morrie*, mentioned earlier, and *Wit*, the Pulitzer Prize–winning play and television movie about learning kindness in the face of terminal cancer. Yet even with such trends in ascendance, there is much work to be done. Physicians today are increasingly reticent to review mistakes at a mortality and morbid-

ity committee, once the traditional setting for medical practitioners to learn from each other in a private forum. Fear of aggressive,
adversarial litigation deters doctors; similarly, accountability measures in education deter educational leaders from talking to one
another about complications and crises. Despite such fears, all crisis
stories, not just those with society's preferred happy ending, offer an
opening for personal and professional growth and deserve a place
in the territory of educational leadership.

A promising and refreshing practice is to be found in "The
Screw-Up Hall of Fame," as described by veteran school head Paul
Bianchi:

> A number of years ago a few teachers and I began a tra-
> dition at Paideia. We established a Screw-Up Hall of
> Fame for faculty and staff. Once a year, usually in the pri-
> vacy of the Board-Faculty Christmas party, we stage a
> pageant where ten finalists from the past twelve months
> are announced and, like a beauty contest, a winner is
> crowned. Throughout the year, nominations from fac-
> ulty and staff pour into my office. I file them in a box on
> my desk discreetly mislabeled "Faculty and Administra-
> tive Issues." Anyone who works for the school is eligible.
> I have won the award twice myself (and am nominated
> with discouraging frequency). We have a plaque listing
> the winners through the years, but we don't display it in
> mixed company. . . . We did not establish the Screw-Up
> Hall of Fame as part of the school's mission statement.
> Nor was it an outgrowth of some overly processed
> administrative initiative. I'm sure the idea came out of
> the faculty lounge on a rainy day when just one too
> many things had gone wrong. But we have kept the tra-
> dition going because it represents an attitude which
> acknowledges that our work is as complicated as life itself

and that the potential for great folly and great achievement fills our days. [Bianchi, 1997, pp. 50–51]

Indeed it does.

Create Circles of Friends

Leaders and organizations would be better served if those responsible for professional development learned to create "circles of friends"
(Hagstrom, 1998–99) who know how to ask open, honest questions
and how to listen deeply. An essential element in any kind of leadership development effort is the safe company of people who are willing to witness each other's stories, without necessarily trying to do
or fix anything. This kind of person-to-person connection can offer
solace, hope, and healing. Safety can come from being with others
who share the burden and vulnerability of leadership. When writing
about his own illness, Albert Schweitzer said that there is a "fellowship of those who bear the mark of pain." Like the medical patient,
wounded leaders would benefit from being with others who understand their brand of pain. Far too many educational leaders do not
have someone to turn to; they are without a safe professional support system. Just as there has been found a relationship between
social isolation and health risk (Goleman, 1995), leadership isolation is detrimental to the health of leaders and their organizations.

When reflecting on his leadership wound and isolation, Carlos
(whose story we heard in Chapter Seven) told us, "I would have
been drowning if I didn't have someone to talk to." He is a survivor
in part because of his support network. He said that he was able to
have the kind of conversation he needed because he had no fear of
retribution or competition with these individuals. He had layers of
support: a principal who worked in the same district and—somewhat
unusual—an assistant superintendent. Since his first year as principal, his circle had expanded to include a university professor from
the opposite side of the country and a principal from Canada, both

members of his professional study group. He told us the study group was formed through an international organization for professional development. Carlos pointed out that he feels safe with each of these caring and competent individuals, yet there are certain matters that he cannot discuss with colleagues within his own district because they are "too close to home," while other issues are actually easier to discuss with them because they are part of the local culture.

Schools, school districts, foundations, and universities are increasingly playing an important role by sponsoring programs and forums for educational leaders to gather and reflect on their practice in the ways described here. Notable today are the principals' centers, leadership academies, and leadership institutes that are steadily emerging and gaining a foothold as integral players in the field of leadership development. The International Network of Principals' Centers (the Network), based at Harvard's Graduate School of Education, has been an active agent in a movement to link centers and foster annual meetings and conversations among leadership centers and school leaders who come from disparate cultures, have unique perspectives, and may even speak different languages but share a common need to talk with each other about school leadership. With communication linkages to support these efforts, a fundamental purpose that the Network holds sacred is the belief that for schools to improve, school leaders must be actively involved in their own and each other's professional development, believing that learning for adults and children in schools can be personal, attractive, and compelling.

In addition, an increasing number of universities require action learning and experiential learning courses, whereby educational leadership students go into the community to help solve real problems, giving them an opportunity to apply skills, collaborate with colleagues, and reflect on their practice in a safe setting (Dilworth, 1998; Dotlich and Noel, 1998; Fulmer, Gibbs, and Goldsmith, 2000; Marquardt, 1999).

At a recent conference, we heard a principal express her wish for a principals' learning community that was "blessed by the district."

As this experienced principal knew, without the approbation of the district it is incredibly hard for principals to justify time spent on themselves. The news is good. An increasing number of schools and school districts are openly and explicitly supporting leaders' efforts to meet, converse, and learn together in new ways. In New York, the Mid-Hudson Leadership Academy of Ulster County BOCES (Board of Cooperative Education Services) is developing a HELP Center (Helping Educational Leaders Persevere) to help school leaders before they find themselves in a crisis situation. Districts and professional developers must continue to seek ways to create time and space for leaders so that they can feel safe to talk, to listen, to wonder, and to dream out loud without worrying about negative exposure or unhealthy competition.

In sum, the need to pay attention to the emotional side of leadership, the need for sustained personal and real conversation among school leaders, and the need for genuine connection and affiliation must be accommodated if leaders are to grow and flourish. "All real living is meeting," Martin Buber reminded us. Leadership is a social and human enterprise; as such, it is essential that there be opportunity for leaders to speak to one another and find meaning behind the dilemmas and crises that are a natural part of their work in schools.

Against our better judgment, we offer some final advice. Here is what to do if you meet a wounded leader crossing the road:

1. Don't ask, "Why did you cross the road?!"
2. Ask, "What is happening now?"
3. Stay in touch with your own fear that you may one day be in the same situation.
4. Ask, "How do you feel about it?"
5. Don't push the person in a direction you might choose yourself.

6. Ask, "What do you want to do about it?"

7. Use your own wounds to develop understanding and compassion.

8. Laugh at fearful things together.

9. Just listen.

Seeking a Cure for Leadership

*Out of the crooked timber of humanity no straight
thing was ever made.*

Immanuel Kant

On the eve of his retirement after fifty years on the job, a wiz-
ened school head said, "A good school must learn to bend
itself around the strengths and vulnerabilities of its leader." What
a genuine challenge for leaders and schools today! Imagine leadership where a leader can show up fully as a person—whole—
strengths, vulnerabilities, and all. Furthermore, imagine a school
with an emotional and intellectual center of gravity spacious
enough to hold not just the leader's virtues and foibles but everyone's in a productive and nurturing orbit. There is increasing evidence to justify placing our hopes in this vision. The final chapter
is a step in that direction.

Imagine this leader:

- I am genuinely interested in learning things, which
  helps others in their attempts to learn.

- I move, sometimes awkwardly, toward understanding
  the leadership position I am in and the responsibilities
  with which I have been entrusted by others.

- I may make mistakes, and I may be inconsistent at times.

- I can talk about my leadership with others.

- I have complicated and sometimes contradictory feelings about power and sharing it.

- I value and respect the dignity of others, yet when I'm fearful I sometimes forget it.

- I try to remain aware of what I need and what others need from my leadership at any particular time.

- I can focus more on challenges at hand rather than expending my energy proving I am something I am not.

- I can use more of my knowledge, skills, and creative imagination in framing and solving problems than in defending myself.

- I can freely change and grow in a leadership position because I am not bound by rigid concepts of what I have been, am now, or ought to be.

- By my own openness and honesty with myself, I can bring out these same qualities in others (thank you, Carl Rogers).

We have sketched some of the qualities of a leadership mind-set implied by all that we have learned in our work with wounded leaders. Each *I* statement in its own way offers a partial promise for thinking anew about the meaning of real leadership and the hope for becoming real in one's leadership. An essential job requirement for this school leader is that she be allowed to be a whole person in her leadership, aware of attitudes that she holds, accepting of her feelings, and real in her relationships with others. Equally important, of course, is that she possess the critical skills and knowledge to lead her and others toward the improvement of teaching and student learning. The qualities and skills embedded in this kind of leadership are not mutually exclusive. We view them as complementary, highly interactive perspectives on fundamental processes of human growth and learning for school leaders.

What does this conception of leadership work mean if applied to the challenges of educational leadership today? American schools and the people who work in them (including and especially school leaders) are increasingly being subjected to and asked to engage in various forms of evaluation and accountability regarding student learning. Standards-based reform has inevitably led to a more vigorous public conversation about the nature of school leadership that can succeed in today's milieu. One response has been to produce an avalanche of innovation and reform. This has brought its own set of victories, some would argue, and even more challenges for school leaders—among them closing the achievement gap between rich and poor schools, getting accountability right for students and adults, improving teaching, and building district and school capacity for leadership. The former dean of the Harvard Graduate School of Education, Jerome T. Murphy, said, "Our expectations have grown much faster than the performance of our schools" (2001, p. 67). Indeed, for many educators and not only school leaders, a kind of weariness (or wariness) has set in as expectation for performance—theirs as well as students'—sometimes far exceeds well-intentioned effort. Some educators feel blamed for problems in schools that are beyond their control. Others feel incompetent. Many school leaders—some admit it, and some don't—do not possess the requisite skills to confront outmoded professional practices and to lead in ways that respond effectively to the increasing demands faced under standards-based reform (Elmore, 2000). The cumulative response for many educators today is collectively and profoundly dispiriting as they negotiate sometimes adversarial and often ambiguous encounters with their public.

These conditions describe a generalized set of challenges for education and for the many excellent school leaders who feel these same challenges in their own wounds. The dissonance so evident in the education profession and in society means good, effective, and well-intentioned leaders must learn to struggle productively with their wounds. The portrait presented here through the lens of the wounded leader is not meant to propose yet another model of leadership, nor is it intended to be overly idealized or romanticized. It just seems to make sense that a person has a solid chance of succeeding in leadership—especially today—because she really knows who she is in a wholehearted way, what she wants to do, what needs doing, and how it might be done. We need this kind of life and energy in our leadership more than ever.

A recurring theme throughout this book is that an important learnable moment for the leader occurs during a wounding crisis, during times of discord. These represent opportunities that, if missed, can have enormous costs, both to the individual leader and to the organization. Ronald Heifetz (1994) suggested that "in a crisis we tend to look for the wrong kind of leadership. We call for someone with answers, decision, strength, and a map of the future . . . in short, someone who can make hard problems simple" (p. 2). He argued that it is actually maladaptive for a group to be "habitually seeking solutions from people in authority" (p. 73). We agree. It is also possible that leaders and schools will adapt to a crisis dysfunctionally. Indeed, many do.

As mentioned previously, many school leaders inevitably become "other centered" (Ackerman, Donaldson, and van der Bogert, 1996), carrying the weight of other people's worries, frustrations, problems, and desires; they then develop their own wounds precisely because they often believe they must hide their fear and vulnerability from others (and quite often from themselves). This was a common issue for school leaders highlighted in the middle chapters.

This book has argued that the school leader suffers from a serious problem that can potentially make leadership itself hazardous to his health; seen through the eyes of the wounded leader, it can be dehumanizing to have a focus that often discounts the meaning of his personal experience—and everyone else's! A healthier approach, reflected in the characteristics of the leader embodied in the portrait we have offered here and developed in a variety of ways throughout the book, is that it is primarily in the awareness of feeling and the inner experience of emotion that a person can discover who she is. Put simply, a school leader, as well as everyone else in a school, has the capacity for developing genuine emotional intelligence and using it effectively. One of the gifts of a keen emotional intelligence (as discussed in Chapter Eleven) is the ability to be responsive in practice to the culture of the school so that, in addition to adapting herself to her organization's culture, the leader is learning to help the culture adapt in ways that allow the culture to flourish for everyone. This kind of leadership requires conscious and skillful development of a supportive environment that learns to manage and adapt to its problems collectively—that is, a culture that truly depends on the knowledge and leadership of the group. Rather than always pointing a finger somewhere else, especially and only toward the leader, the school can be remolded to reflect a culture of shared responsibility for what happens, as well as what does not happen.

There are educational institutions and leaders moving and learning their way tentatively in this direction. The critical element in these approaches is that the leaders and leadership itself are being understood in a more personal and real way. Operating from this reconfigured role means the leader is given permission to acknowledge limitations and can be open about reaching out for what is needed to lead effectively. As brought out in the stories in this book, leaders often believe that they are supposed to be helpers and fixers, as well as independent and strong, the same qualities that can thwart them from listening to their own needs. To be sure, traditional criteria for judging leadership effectiveness continue to dominate the leadership landscapes of preparation, in-service, and practice: "be right," "be in control," "be invulnerable," "be rational," and even "be liked," to name a few. To redefine these criteria would signal a sea change in our understanding of leadership knowledge, responsibility, caring, information, and conflict, respectively. Put differently, to accept one's separateness and honor that of others, to inquire through interaction and a genuine search for questions and answers, to take responsibility for oneself but not the thoughts and feelings of others or the forces over which one has no control, and to confront and use authority as the ultimate expression of caring are all signals of real leadership.

The changing norms of schooling are giving way to new leadership forms; there is emerging advocacy for such forms—teacher leadership, for example—viewing the work of leadership as, integrally, the conscious, active, and deliberate "cultivation" (Donaldson, 2001) of leadership in schools. Leadership today needs to survive and in fact flourish on the basis of two fundamental assumptions and practices: there are many qualified people under the schoolhouse roof who want and need to be involved in leadership work, and schools and districts must be actively involved in helping to grow their own leaders to do that work. This represents a different and promising way of thinking about leadership in schools. It is also a new way of thinking about roles and responsibilities and the possibility that schools can really take on new ways of leading themselves. As such, school organizations and communities may begin to look and behave more like ecosystems where more have access to the whole, and people support and nurture one another with trust.

A large conversation is taking shape today within our emerging educational ecosystems, in part thanks to an ever-expanding variety of technologies permitting individuals, as well as schools, to communicate and share information and knowledge with each other in a timely, instantaneous way and at blinding speed. The advent of this exciting technology poses even more adaptive challenges to educators who place a high value on natural, open, and honest communication. Clearly, we must remember to keep our own human voices unmistakably real in the so-called information age so we can enable and nurture humane organizational structures, forms, and, especially, leadership that remains passionately committed to human learning in all its infinite variety.

We hope this book makes the case for a climate of trust and openness in leadership, in which curiosity and the natural desire to learn can be nourished and enhanced by all members of an educational community. It aims toward helping leaders value themselves, and toward uncovering the spirit in emotional discovery that leads the leader to become a lifelong learner. It looks toward helping the leader grow as a person; even more deeply, it aims toward an awareness that the work of genuine leadership is not something dependent on outside sources but instead within all of us.

Ultimately, there is no absolute cure for leadership wounding, or simple formula for leadership survival. Real leadership is in the end a very personal matter. Our hope is that crisis stories can be honored and leaders can be supported in their quest for personal and professional growth so that schools can also evolve, change as necessary, and improve learning for all. Our wish is that the leader continues to reach for a dream shared by educators around the world—that every student develops to his or her fullest potential—and works to make that dream come true. That's what we call a good story.

Appendix A:
Method of Inquiry

This text represents the work of an ongoing research agenda seeking to elucidate how leaders cope with and respond to dilemma and crisis in practice. Our interest is in understanding what this kind of experience means to educational leaders and how it influences their professional as well as personal growth and development. An important corollary interest is in what this means to the organization. In the context of this book, however, we have focused on how a wounding crisis serves as a catalyst for change and how it becomes (or does not become) an impetus to question the very foundation of one's leadership.

We designed a series of four phenomenological studies using leaders' first-person accounts of their experience with crisis to explore what it means to be a wounded leader and to identify implications for leadership development. Our interpretation and reflections on the findings across these studies are the basis of *The Wounded Leader*.

Research Leading to Wounded Leader Study

The research background for this book is a line of investigation into leaders and crisis that has progressed over a period of seven years. Three early studies of how leaders use story to make sense of their practice brought us to the idea of a wounded leader (Ackerman and

Maslin-Ostrowski, 1995, 1997; Maslin-Ostrowski and Ackerman, 1997). The combined sample for these three leadership studies consisted of 215 prospective and practicing leaders. Our quest began with a comparative study of the case study method and an approach we call case story.

Continuing this line of inquiry, our next study examined how school leaders learn to think together—not just in the sense of analyzing a shared dilemma or issue but in how story forms shape meaning for groups of people and lead to a kind of critical conversation (Brookfield, 1995) through which thoughts, emotions, and actions fit into a greater whole.

This led to our third study, in which we began to speculate that in many instances, the case story groups have the potential to develop a kind of host system of social, cognitive, and emotional structures for nurturing the capacity to pay attention to the meaning of individual experience and its power to instruct. Most conversations required retelling and revelation of the experience; they inevitably created a return to a level of feeling and emotion that the original experience engendered. In short, telling the stories invariably returned to some of the heat that was part of the original conflict. The individual and collective quest to make sense of complex reality through case story was found to be critical to the learning that emerged for our participants. The case story may serve an important purpose, integrating personal experience with administrative theory; it is here that we found leaders stepping beyond conventional language and expression and engaging in what we have come to think of as courageous conversation.

Reflecting on these three studies, we redirected our research somewhat as we began to see striking similarity between the stories leaders were telling about crisis in practice and those of individuals confronting a medical illness. This led us to explore the literatures about illness experience and ethics, as in the writings of Arthur Frank, Arthur Kleinman, and Rachel Remen, among others. Our emerging idea of wounded leaders was crystallized.

Purpose and Design of the Study

This phenomenological study, completed in four stages, was an effort to listen our way into the worlds of public and private school administrators who were identified as having experienced a crisis or critical event in their leadership practice that had profoundly affected or wounded them, to understand the essence of their wounding experience.

The purpose of the first study was to understand how significant leadership crisis creates a particular context for telling a story, and specifically how the life of the school leaders is affected by the story told. We were interested not just in the explicit content of the stories—the actions, events, and responses—but also in how these leader stories served to address the woundedness of the leaders and helped them, in a sense, to heal themselves. Our second study added a new focus: What are the wounds of school leaders? How do they understand them, and what are the barriers that prevent them from seeing their wounds?

With the findings of these studies in mind, our third investigation expanded to explore what school leaders learn from their wounds, and how educational leadership preparation and professional development programs might better support their growth. The fourth and final study in this series sought to understand the emotional dimensions of becoming a wounded leader.

To address these questions, we designed an interview study using the leader's first-person account of an experience with crisis as the primary source of information. Located within the broad perspective of qualitative research, the study was phenomenological (Moustakas, 1994; Polkinghorne, 1989) in that it focused on the individual leader's meaning of the phenomenon or experience of being wounded. The four studies conducted over time allowed us to direct our analysis toward different questions each time, while also extending analysis of prior questions (Maslin-Ostrowski and Ackerman, 1998b, 2000a, 2000b; Ackerman and Maslin-Ostrowski, 2001).

It was not feasible to conduct observations; nor did we see merit in doing much with document analysis. (Documents were used simply to produce a profile of the school sites and, when possible, to extend our understanding of the crisis. This included demographic information, school literature, and at times newspaper articles about the school and administration.) Thus the study used a single method for data collection—interviews—which is a limitation.

Sampling Plan

The overall purposeful sample for the four wounded leader studies consisted of sixty-five educational leaders who have dealt with a significant crisis in their own leadership practice. We targeted superintendents, principals, and heads of independent schools. Our sample was far from random. The first set of seven leaders was found through our personal network of contacts. Then, using referrals from those participants and from colleagues around the country, the sample expanded.

We first spoke with leaders to introduce our study, usually over the telephone, and to make arrangements to meet in person. They were invited to think about and choose a crisis experience that had affected them significantly and that they would be willing to discuss. No one that we approached had any difficulty identifying such an experience; however, sometimes the experience selected was not the one we anticipated on the basis of information from the referral source. Some participants knew instantly what they wanted to talk about, while others said they needed to think about which experience to share for the interview.

Participants came from a variety of school contexts (elementary, middle, and high school) and represented public and private institutions. They worked and lived in urban, suburban, and rural settings located in various regions of the country. The majority came from the eastern seaboard. Leaders served communities that were diverse in terms of socioeconomic status, race, and ethnicity. The small number of cases is a study limitation. To increase our sample, for each subsequent study we included all interviews from prior wounded leader studies. A future study using a larger sample with greater variation may yield additional insights into leaders and wounding experiences.

Leader Interviews

For all interviews, we used a simple interview guide and asked open-ended questions that directed the participant toward our line of inquiry. A few open-ended questions rather than a standardized set of questions were posed. Our intent was to facilitate narrative telling and not to interfere with the participant's responses. Thus the discourse of an interview was conversational, not standardized questioning. By abandoning the question-and-answer format, we made room for the participant to respond at length and to narrate her experience in her own way. We tried to create an interview environment that allowed the storyteller to make sense of her experience as we listened. For example, we did not rush participants, instead letting them speak at great length without interruption. This one-to-one, in-depth approach to interviewing was appropriate because it supported telling personal, sensitive experiences and perspectives.

All interviews were audiotaped and later carefully transcribed, incorporating the words of both participant and interviewer. Demographic information about the participants and their school settings was collected through the interviews, as well as from documents. Confidentiality was promised to each participant. Because of the sensitive nature of the stories, we agreed to change names and places when using a narrator's words to ensure privacy, yet never at the expense of the meaning of what he or she said.

For the first study, with some variation to accommodate the school leader's schedule and time constraints, three interviews were held with each of the seven participants over a period of nine months; each interview was ninety minutes to two hours in length (Seidman, 1991). One basic open-ended question was asked at each interview. During the initial interview a narrator was invited to reconstruct his or her life and career history, telling about past experience as an educator up to the point of the crisis. This encouraged the narrator to provide a personal context for stories told in subsequent interviews.

In the second interview, the participant was asked to focus on the details of the critical event or significant experience. Each narrator was asked to reconstruct the experience and tell what happened. Finally, in the third interview the narrator was asked to reflect on what was said in the first two interviews, and to talk about what that meant in terms of who the individual is today as a leader and as a person. They were also invited to reflect on how they presently understand leadership in their lives. What unfolded in the participants' narrative accounts was a combination of a chronology of events and an attempt to give meaning to events.

Again applying an in-depth, phenomenological approach to interviewing, we conducted interviews for the second, third, and fourth studies wherein we invited each participant to construct or reconstruct his or her wounding experience. (The fourth study conducted follow-up interviews exclusively; sample size did not change.) Given the growing sample size and knowledge gained from the first study, interviews now ranged in length from one to three hours. With some participants, we conducted multiple interviews. Our aim was to learn how school leaders dealt with a self-identified crisis as it had affected their professional lives then and now, why they had decided to follow a particular course of action, and what the outcome was. Naturally, along the way we were told a good deal about how events affected the leaders' personal lives as well. Overwhelmingly, leaders chose to talk about a "living crisis," no matter how far in the past the crisis occurred. Our interest was in understanding the stories that they were telling themselves and what the narrative meant to them as leaders.

Story Analysis

We regularly alternated between data collection and data analysis. Data gathered and analyzed during one phase of the study influenced collection of data from subsequent participants. During analysis, our focus was on both what the school leaders said and how they formed their stories. We were interested in how they told their point of view and perception of the experience. With this in mind, we analyzed each participant's story as a narrative entity; that is, stories were kept intact.

After transcribing the audiotaped interviews, we carefully read and reread the stories to see how the participant had given order to a difficult experience and made sense of the event. We also listened to the tapes repeatedly to hear the nuances and ambiguities of oral language and document significant features, such as long pauses, laughter, and so forth. The goal of data analysis was not simply to identify what had happened but to understand why participants told their story the way they did. Thus we attempted to look at these stories and consider how the interviewee made meaning, rather than fracturing stories into small categories. We examined each story as a narrative form that was not dissected into parts and separated from the whole.

Although we were interested in how people use story to think about their leadership wounds, we did not conduct a narrative analysis of text and linguistic structures in the detailed manner that others have used (see Riessman, 1993).

Applying investigator triangulation, two researchers independently collected and analyzed all data until findings emerged and consensus was reached. After carefully reviewing the rich sample of stories, we decided to employ a specific narrative typology found in the work of Arthur Frank (1995). The typology consists of three narrative types: the quest, restitution, and chaos story. We found this typology useful in that it offered a way to think about and talk about wounded leaders' narrative identity and how they made meaning of crisis experience.

Member checking was completed to enhance internal validity, whereby participants were given the opportunity to read or check the transcripts and respond to our interpretation of what we heard (Lincoln and Guba, 1985). We strived for mutual interpretation during the actual interview and afterward with any follow-up session. Conclusions were based on the stories, along with consideration of alternative interpretations.

What distinguishes the wounded leader study was the participatory nature of the relationship we established with our narrators (Bosk, 1979). We concluded that insights gleaned from the study were in part the result of our relationship and that a research method divorced from our interests, purposes, and values, as well as theirs, was neither possible nor desirable. The fieldwork for this study thus was mediated by our experience and that of the informant, a point that has been made by a number of fieldworkers in recent years (Mishler, 1986). To appreciate fully the meaning of behavior and perception, as well as to identify our own bias, required a research strategy that developed as trust and self-disclosure deepened. We paid particular attention to how our own presence and bias affected the research setting (Hammersley and Atkinson, 1983), using the opportunity to analyze the meaning of our presence for and with participants. Along these lines, we were open with the participant about being personally interested in both the individual story and our research project.

Furthermore, because we are two researchers collaborating, we co-interpreted the stories. Given that all interviews were conducted one-on-one, only one of us was present, and only one of us consequently had a relationship with the participant. This meant that the researcher who conducted the interview had a tremendous responsibility to portray accurately and honestly the authenticity of the leader's emotions, ideas, and interpretations of the wounding experience. We have tried our best to honor that commitment. From our view, the collaboration helped to recognize bias and enhanced researcher discourse; thus it is a strength of the study. The research design therefore required a perspective in which methodology, data, and theory were mutually informing.

Appendix B: Case Story

A case story is a description, both written and oral, of a real-life, close-to-the-bone leadership situation, written with words meant to come fully to life when discussed. In contrast to the familiar case study, in which the participant learns vicariously through other people's cases, the case story approach invites people to learn through writing and telling their own personal experience as practitioners. A case story, then, blends aspects of the case study method (Christensen and Hansen, 1987) with the tradition, artistry, and imagination of story (Campbell, 1968; Campbell and Moyers, 1988) and storytelling (Egan, 1989).

We and others have used case story in a variety of settings: leadership institutes, professional development programs, workshops, and graduate-level classrooms. The case story model, presented here, requires a minimum of three hours to implement and includes five steps that are simply outlined here (see also Ackerman, Maslin-Ostrowski, and Christensen, 1996; Maslin-Ostrowski and Ackerman, 1998a). The approach works best if there is a skilled facilitator who helps create a safe, positive learning atmosphere and who gently guides the participant through each step of the case story writing and storytelling process.

Case Story Model

Step One: The Free Write

The "free write" activity is designed to warm the participant to writing about issues of practice and leadership. Everyone is asked to write for seven minutes using a stem such as "The obstacle to leadership for me is . . ." After writing, participants are divided into groups of three to read aloud and talk about their free writes.

Step Two: Writing Case Stories

After the facilitator provides explicit directions and shares an example, participants are invited to write a one-page case story that describes a real-life, close-to-the-bone leadership dilemma or critical incident, one that remains unresolved in their mind.

Step Three: Telling, Listening to, and Discussing Case Stories

In triads, participants are guided to take turns telling, listening to, and discussing case stories. The conversation is carefully structured so that the storyteller reads and elaborates on his story without interruption, followed by a moment of silence. Next, there is discussion of his story, which initially he observes and listens to before joining the dialogue. Giving advice is forbidden. The goal is not to find a single solution or to fix the problem, but rather to examine alternatives and consider the consequences, and to ask and reflect on good, genuine questions. Although expressing feelings about the problem or trauma is cathartic and can even be helpful, the ultimate goal is for the storyteller to find meaning in the difficult experience.

Step Four: Small-Group Reflection

Triads are merged into groups of six, where participants are asked to consider what the experience of hearing others' stories was like, as well as to reflect on what it was like to share and discuss their own case stories.

Step Five: Whole-Group Reflection

The small groups are asked to report important findings. The entire group is then invited to reflect on their learning experience.

References

Ackerman, R. H., Donaldson, G., Jr., and van der Bogert, R. *Making Sense as a School Leader*. San Francisco: Jossey-Bass, 1996.

Ackerman, R. H., and Maslin-Ostrowski, P. "Developing Case Stories: An Analysis of the Case Method of Instruction and Storytelling in Teaching Educational Administration." Paper presented at annual meeting of the American Educational Research Association, San Francisco, Apr. 1995.

Ackerman, R. H., and Maslin-Ostrowski, P. "Real Talk: Understanding Case Story in Teaching Educational Leadership." In H. E. Klein (ed.), *Interactive Teaching and Learning: Case Method and Other Techniques*. Boston: World Association for Case Method Research and Application, 1997.

Ackerman, R. H., and Maslin-Ostrowski, P. "The Emotional Landscape: Lessons from Wounded Leaders." Paper presented at annual meeting of the American Educational Research Association, Seattle, Apr. 2001.

Ackerman, R. H., Maslin-Ostrowski, P., and Christensen, C. "Case Stories: Telling Tales About School." *Educational Leadership*, 1996, *53*(6), 21–24.

Alan, D., Blythe, T., and Powell, B. "A Guide to Looking Collaboratively at Student Work: An Essential Toolkit." Providence, R.I.: Coalition of Essential Schools, 2001.

Albom, M. *Tuesdays with Morrie: An Old Man, a Young Man, and Life's Great Lesson*. New York: Doubleday, 1997.

Argyris, C. *Strategy, Change, and Defensive Routines*. New York: Ballinger, 1985.

Argyris, C. *Personality and Organization*. New York: Garland, 1987.

Argyris, C., and Schön, D. *Theory in Practice: Increasing Professional Effectiveness*. San Francisco: Jossey-Bass, 1974.

Armstrong, L., and Jenkins, S. *It's Not About the Bike: My Journey Back to Life*. New York: Putnam, 2000.

Barth, R. *Improving Schools from Within: Teachers, Parents, and Principals Can Make the Difference*. San Francisco: Jossey-Bass, 1990.

Bauby, J.-D. *The Diving Bell and the Butterfly*. New York: Knopf, 1997.

Bennis, W. G. *On Becoming a Leader*. Reading, Mass.: Addison-Wesley, 1989.

Bianchi, P. "There's No Doubt We're Alive." In G. A. Donaldson, Jr. (ed.), *On Being a Principal: The Rewards and Challenges of School Leadership*. New Directions for School Leadership, no. 5. San Francisco: Jossey-Bass, 1997.

Bosk, C. *Forgive and Remember: Managing Medical Failure*. Chicago: University of Chicago Press, 1979.

Brinton, H. H. *Quaker Education in Theory and Practice*. (Pendlehill pamphlet no. 9.) Wallingford, Pa.: Pendlehill, 1940.

Brookfield, S. D. *Becoming a Critically Reflective Teacher*. San Francisco: Jossey-Bass, 1995.

Bruner, J. *Actual Minds, Possible Worlds*. Cambridge, Mass.: Harvard University Press, 1986.

Bruner, J. "Life as Narrative." *Social Research*, 1987, *54*, 11–32.

Callahan, R. *Education and the Cult of Efficiency: A Study of the Social Forces That Have Shaped the Administration of the Public Schools*. Chicago: University of Chicago Press, 1962.

Campbell, J. *The Hero with a Thousand Faces*. New York: MJF Books, 1949.

Campbell, J. *The Masks of God*, Vol. 4: *Creative Mythology*. New York: Viking, 1968.

Campbell, J., and Moyers, B. *The Power of Myth*. New York: Doubleday, 1988.

Carmichael, L. "Working Within the Authority Pyramid." *Education and Urban Society*, 1985, *17*(3), 311–323.

Chödrön, P. *The Places That Scare You: A Guide to Fearlessness in Difficult Times*. Boston: Shambhala, 2001.

Christensen, C. R., and Hansen, A. J. *Teaching and the Case Method: Text, Cases, and Readings*. Boston: Harvard Business School Press, 1987.

Clandinin, D. J., and Connelly, F. M. "Story of Experience and Narrative Inquiry." *Educational Researcher*, 1990, *19*(5), 2–14.

Coles, R. *The Call of Stories: Teaching and the Moral Imagination*. Boston: Houghton Mifflin, 1989.

Collett, M. *Stay Close and Do Nothing: A Spiritual and Practical Guide to Caring for the Dying*. Kansas City, Mo.: Andrews McMeel, 1997.

Cooper, P. K., and Sawaf, A. *Executive EQ: Emotional Intelligence in Leadership and Organizations*. New York: Perigee, 1997.

Cousins, N. *Anatomy of an Illness as Perceived by the Patient.* New York: Norton, 1979.

Damasio, A. *Descartes' Error: Emotion, Reason, and the Human Brain.* New York: Putnam, 1994.

Damasio, A. *The Feeling of What Happens: Body and Emotion in the Making of Consciousness.* Orlando: Harcourt Brace, 1999.

Dewey, J. *Experience and Education.* New York: Collier, Macmillan, 1963. (Originally published 1938.)

Diamond, J. *Because Cowards Get Cancer Too: A Hypochondriac Confronts His Nemesis.* New York: Random House, 1998.

Dilworth, R. L. "Action Learning in a Nutshell." *Performance Improvement Quarterly,* 1998, *11*(1), 28–43.

Donaldson, G., Jr. *Cultivating Leadership in School: Connecting People, Purpose, and Practice.* New York: Teachers College Press, 2001.

Donaldson, G., Jr., and Marnik, G. F. *Becoming Better Leaders: The Challenge of Improving Student Learning.* Thousand Oaks, Calif.: Corwin Press, 1995.

Dotlich, D. L., and Noel, J. L. *Action Learning: How the World's Top Companies Are Recreating Their Leaders and Themselves.* San Francisco: Jossey-Bass, 1998.

Egan, K. *Teaching as Storytelling.* Chicago: University of Chicago Press, 1989.

Egan, K. *Imagination in Teaching and Learning: The Middle School Years.* Chicago: University of Chicago Press, 1992.

Eisner, E. *The Educational Imagination: On the Design and Evaluation of School Programs.* (2nd ed.) New York: Macmillan, 1985.

Elbaz, F. "Knowledge and Discourse: The Evolution of Research on Teacher Thinking." In C. Day, P. Denicolo, and M. Pope (eds.), *Insights into Teachers' Thinking and Practice.* London: Falmer, 1990.

Elmore, R. "Building a New Structure for School Leadership." Washington, D.C.: Albert Shanker Institute, Winter 2000.

Evans, R. *The Human Side of School Change: Reform, Resistance, and the Real-Life Problems of Innovation.* San Francisco: Jossey-Bass, 1996.

Frank, A. *At the Will of the Body: Reflections on Illness.* Boston: Houghton Mifflin, 1991.

Frank, A. *The Wounded Storyteller: Body, Illness, and Ethics.* Chicago: University of Chicago Press, 1995.

Fullan, M. "Breaking the Bonds of Dependency." *Educational Leadership,* 1998, *55*(7), 6–10.

Fullan, M., and Miles, M. "Getting Reform Right: What Works and What Doesn't." *Phi Delta Kappan,* 1992, *73*(10), 744–754.

Fulmer, R. M., Gibbs, P. S., and Goldsmith, M. "Developing Leaders: How Winning Companies Keep on Winning." *Sloan Management Review*, 2000, 42(1), 49–59.

Gardner, H. *Frames of Mind: The Theory of Multiple Intelligences*. New York: Basic Books, 1993.

Gardner, H. *Leading Minds: An Anatomy of Leadership*. New York: Basic Books, 1995.

Goleman, D. *Emotional Intelligence: Why It Can Matter More Than IQ*. New York: Bantam, 1995.

Goleman, D. *Working with Emotional Intelligence*. New York: Bantam, 1998.

Groopman, J. E. *The Measure of Our Days: A Spiritual Exploration of Illness*. New York: Penguin, 1997.

Grumet, M. *Bitter Milk: Women and Teaching*. Amherst: University of Massachusetts Press, 1988.

Hagstrom, D. "Seeking Clarity About Crisis." *Educational Leadership*, 1998–99, 56(4), 53–57.

Hallowell, B. "My Nonnegotiables." In G. A. Donaldson, Jr. (ed.), *On Being a Principal: The Rewards and Challenges of School Leadership*. New Directions for School Leadership, no. 5. San Francisco: Jossey-Bass, 1997.

Hammersley, M., and Atkinson, P. *Ethnography: Principles in Practice*. London: Tavistock, 1983.

Hardy, B. "Narrative as a Primary Act of Mind." In M. Meek, A. A. Warlow, and G. Barton (eds.), *The Cool Web*. London: Bodley Head, 1977.

Heifetz, R. A. *Leadership Without Easy Answers*. Cambridge, Mass.: Belknap Press, 1994.

Hillman, J. *Emotion: A Comprehensive Phenomenology of Theories and Their Meanings for Therapy*. Evanston, Ill.: Northwestern University Press, 1997.

Huberman, M. "Working with Life-History Narratives." In H. McEwan and K. Egan (eds.), *Narrative in Teaching, Learning, and Research*. New York: Teachers College Press, 1995.

Isaacs, W. *Dialogue and the Art of Thinking Together*. New York: Currency Doubleday, 1999.

Jackson, P. W. "Lonely at the Top: Observations on the Genesis of Administrative Isolation." Revised version of paper read at annual meeting of American Educational Research Association, San Francisco, Apr. 1976.

Jackson, P. W. "On the Place of Narrative in Teaching." In H. McEwan and K. Egan (eds.), *Narrative in Teaching, Learning, and Research*. New York: Teachers College Press, 1995.

James, T. *Education at the Edge: The Colorado Outward Bound School.* Denver: Colorado Outward Bound School, 1980.

Jentz, B. C., and Wofford, J. W. *Leadership and Learning: Personal Change in a Professional Setting.* New York: McGraw-Hill, 1979.

Johnson, R. A. *The Fisher King and the Handless Maiden: Understanding the Wounded Feeling Function in Masculine and Feminine Psychology.* San Francisco: Harper San Francisco, 1993.

Johnson, R. *Owning Your Own Shadow: Understanding the Dark Side of the Psyche.* New York: HarperCollins, 1991.

Jung, E., and Franz, M.-L. *The Grail Legend.* Princeton, N.J.: Princeton University Press, 1970.

Kegan, R., and Lahey, L. *How the Way We Talk Can Change the Way We Work: Seven Languages for Transformation.* San Francisco: Jossey-Bass, 2001.

Kets de Vries, M. *Leaders, Fools, and Imposters: Essays on the Psychology of Leadership.* San Francisco: Jossey-Bass, 1993.

Kleinman, A. *The Illness Narratives: Suffering, Healing, and the Human Condition.* New York: Basic Books, 1988.

Lambert, L. *Building Leadership Capacity in Schools.* Alexandria, Va.: Association for Supervision and Curriculum Development, 1998.

Lave, J. "The Practice of Learning." In S. Chaiklin and J. Lave (eds.), *Understanding Practice: Perspectives on Activity and Context.* Cambridge, England: Cambridge University Press, 1996.

Lave, J., and Wenger, E. *Situated Learning: Legitimate Peripheral Participation.* Cambridge, England: Cambridge University Press, 1991.

Lincoln, Y., and Guba, E. *Naturalistic Inquiry.* Thousand Oaks, Calif.: Sage, 1985.

Lutz, F., and Wisener, B. "Vulnerability of Humankind." *Peabody Journal of Education,* 1996, *71*(2), 86–95.

Marquardt, M. J. *Action Learning in Action: Transforming Problems and People for World-Class Organizational Learning.* Palo Alto, Calif.: Davies-Black, 1999.

Maslin-Ostrowski, P., and Ackerman, R. H. "A Case for Stories: Toward Further Understanding of Situated Knowledge and Practice." Paper presented at annual meeting of the American Educational Research Association, Chicago, Apr. 1997.

Maslin-Ostrowski, P., and Ackerman, R. "Case Story." In M. W. Galbraith (ed.), *Adult Learning Methods: A Guide for Effective Instruction.* (2nd ed.) Malabar, Fla.: Krieger, 1998a.

Maslin-Ostrowski, P., and Ackerman, R. H. "The Wounded Leader: Looking for the Good Story." Paper presented at annual meeting of the American Educational Research Association, San Diego, Apr. 1998b.

Maslin-Ostrowski, P., and Ackerman, R. H. "On Being Wounded: Implications for School Leadership." *Journal of Educational Administration*, 2000a, *38*(3), 1–11.

Maslin-Ostrowski, P., and Ackerman, R. H. *"The Wounded Leader: Implications for Educational Leadership Preparation and Professional Development."* Paper presented at annual meeting of the American Educational Research Association, New Orleans, Apr. 2000b.

MacIntyre, A. *After Virtue*. Notre Dame, Ind.: University of Notre Dame Press, 1981.

McCrum, R. *My Year Off: Recovering Life After a Stroke*. New York: Norton, 1998.

McClelland, D. *Power: The Inner Experience*. New York: Irvington, 1975.

McDonald, J. *Redesigning School: Lessons for the 21st Century*. San Francisco: Jossey-Bass, 1996.

Mezirow, J. *Transformative Dimensions of Adult Learning*. San Francisco: Jossey-Bass, 1991.

Mishler, E. G. *Research Interviewing: Context and Narrative*. Cambridge, Mass.: Harvard University Press, 1986.

Moller, G., and Katzenmeyer, D. (eds.). *Every Teacher a Leader: Realizing the Potential of Teacher Leadership*. New Directions for School Leadership, no. 1. San Francisco: Jossey-Bass, 1996.

Moustakas, C. *Phenomenological Research Methods*. Thousand Oaks, Calif.: Sage, 1994.

Murphy, J. T. "Education Agendas." *Harvard*, 2001, *103*(6), 67.

NASBE Study Group on School Leadership. *What Education Leaders Need to Lead Schools to Excellence*. Alexandria and Reston, Va.: National Association of State Boards of Education, 1999.

National Association of Elementary School Principals. *Leading Learning Communities: Standards for What Principals Should Know and Be Able to Do*. Alexandria, Va.: NAESP, 2001.

Nouwen, H. *The Wounded Healer*. New York: Image, 1990.

Palmer, P. J. *The Courage to Teach: Exploring the Inner Landscape of a Teacher's Life*. San Francisco: Jossey-Bass, 1998.

Palmer, P. J. *Let Your Life Speak: Listening for the Voice of Vocation*. San Francisco: Jossey-Bass, 2000.

Polkinghorne, D. E. *Narrative Knowing and the Human Sciences*. Albany: State University of New York Press, 1988.

Polkinghorne, D. E. "Phenomenological Research Methods." In R. S. Valle and S. Halling (eds.), *Existential-Phenomenological Perspectives in Psychology*. New York: Plenum, 1989.

Post, G., and Robins, R. S. *When Illness Strikes the Leader: The Dilemma of the Captive King*. New Haven: Yale University Press, 1993.

Radner, G. *It's Always Something*. New York: Avon, 1989.

Remen, R. N. *Kitchen Table Wisdom: Stories That Heal*. New York: Riverhead, 1996.

Remen, R. N. *My Grandfather's Blessings: Stories of Strength, Refuge, and Belonging*. New York: Riverhead, 2000.

Ricoeur, P. *Time and Narrative*. Chicago: University of Chicago Press, 1984.

Riessman, C. K. *Narrative Analysis*. Thousand Oaks, Calif.: Sage, 1993.

Rogers, C. R. *On Becoming a Person: A Therapist's View of Psychotherapy*. Boston: Houghton Mifflin, 1961.

Sacks, O. *A Leg to Stand On*. New York: Touchstone, 1998.

Sarbin, T. (ed.). *Narrative Psychology: The Storied Nature of Human Conduct*. New York: Praeger, 1986.

Schaefer, R. *Retelling a Life: Narration and Dialogue in Psychoanalysis*. New York: Basic Books, 1992.

Seidman, I. E. *Interviewing as Qualitative Research: A Guide for Researchers in Education and the Social Sciences*. New York: Teachers College Press, 1991.

Snyder, K. J., Acker-Hocevar, M., and Snyder, K. M. *Living on the Edge of Chaos: Leading Schools into the Global Age*. Milwaukee, Wis.: ASQ Quality Press, 2000.

Sontag, S. *Illness as Metaphor*. New York: Vintage, 1978.

Strauss, A. *Qualitative Analysis for Social Scientists*. New York: Cambridge University Press, 1987.

Verghese, A. *My Own Country: A Doctor's Story*. New York: Vintage, 1995.

Walsh, V., and Golins, G. *The Exploration of Outward Bound Process*. Denver: Outward Bound School, 1976.

Weston, J. *From Ritual to Romance*. New York: Dover, 1993. (Originally published 1907.)

Whyte, D. *The Heart Aroused: Poetry and the Preservation of the Soul in Corporate America*. New York: Doubleday, 1994.

Whyte, D. *Crossing the Unknown Sea: Work as a Pilgrimage of Identity*. New York: Riverhead, 2001.

Witherell, C., and Noddings, N. *Stories Lives Tell: Narrative and Dialogue in Education*. New York: Teachers College Press, 1991.

Witherell, C., Tran, H., and Othus, J. "Narrative Landscapes and the Moral Imagination." In McEwan and Egan (eds.), *Narrative in Teaching, Learning, and Research*. New York: Teachers College Press, 1995.

Index